KEYS

of

DECEPTION

His Game with NO Remorse

BECCA JOY BAILEY

ISBN:
eBook: 979-8-9917126-0-6
Paperback: 979-8-9917126-1-3
Hardback: 979-8-9917126-2-0

CONTENTS

This book is dedicated to my precious and courageous daughter. She has endured more than I had ever wished she had to, yet I feel certain she is stronger and wiser because of our life experiences. I greatly admire her. She is a gift from God, and I will always be thankful for her.

Prologue: The Envelope

The frigid wind blew the hair away from my face as I sprinted down the driveway to get my mail. I was not prepared for what I was about to find. The second I saw our names together on the envelope, my knees nearly buckled, and I almost collapsed. So many years had passed, but this brought it crashing back as vividly as if it had happened yesterday.

I carried the envelope back to my house, wondering why our names graced the same piece of paper, not even daring to guess as to what it could contain. I stood in the entryway, my hands shaking, but not from the freezing temperatures. I tore through the envelope, the paper slicing my finger open, adding injury to the insult.

The formally typed letter from the bank offered an apology for freezing my accounts almost fifteen years ago. Accompanying the letter was a check for $100. It was all I could do to not tear up the money, never mind how much I needed it. The shame and pain of his betrayal burned deep inside of me.

PART 1 – THE BEGINNING

Chapter 1

THE FIRE

1966

When I was in first grade, we lived in a five-bedroom brick home that was nine miles out of town. One December morning soon after Christmas, I remember vividly waking up to my sister Caitlin's shrill screams, "Get up! Get up! The house is on fire!"

Her room had been closest to the fire, and she woke up first. It was over fifty years ago, but I remember it as if it were yesterday. The overpowering smoke made it hard to breathe without coughing, and it was so thick, it was difficult to see down the hallway toward our brother Reagan's room. We held onto the walls to guide us through the smoke-filled house. I grabbed hold of Caitlin's hand as tight as possible, not wanting to let go. She had always been my protective big sister.

In Reagan's room, he woke quickly, the fear showing in his eyes. Then we ran together to our parents' room. Flames were building higher and higher in every direction and the smoke billowed around us.

It is strange how your mind can expand every second to seem like minutes when you're in danger, and it felt like everything was in slow motion. As fast as we were trying to reach Mom and Daddy, it still seemed to take forever, as if it were a mirage. Once we finally were in their bedroom, Mom was hard to rouse. We did not have a minute to spare.

We kept shaking her and yelling, "Mom, wake up! Our house is on fire! Please wake up!" Reagan's blond curls shook as he jumped on the bed, pulling the covers off. Reagan's determination was clear; he wanted us all out of the house safely, especially Mom. Finally, she woke up coughing, then realized we were in danger.

Daddy scurried to put on his pants and looked for his car keys. He soon found them in the bathroom, then led us down the hall and to the back door to safety. We were all barefoot, since we'd run out of the house without time to grab shoes or any of our belongings.

The intense heat had broken glass, and fire billowed out of the windows and through the roof. The curtains were lying on the snow-covered grass as we ran across the back lawn. My feet felt frozen as we hurried through the gate to get in Daddy's car.

Mom surprised us all when she cried out, "I need my robe. I want the kids' pictures, our family pictures, ALL of our pictures! What about Princess?" Our German Shepherd was nowhere to be seen.

Mom ran toward the house, but before she reached the door, Daddy grabbed her and said, "No, it's too dangerous! We can't go back inside for anything. We've gotta go now!"

Daddy was a gentle man who rarely raised his voice for any reason, but his voice was louder than I ever remembered! Even as a little girl, I knew he was scared. I was so relieved when Mom turned away and we continued our trek through the burning debris and smoky backyard. Everything was lit up by the bright security light that shone over the backyard, accentuating the pitch-black sky, the playhouse, and the shed.

Daddy's blue Buick was parked just outside of the garage, and we all ran toward it, my father rushing us along, making sure we were all together. Mom, Caitlin, and I climbed in the backseat, and Mom just kept holding us, saying over and over, "It will be okay. It will be okay. It will be okay."

I knew from her trembling voice and the tears in her eyes that it was not okay. It was far from being okay. I wanted to believe it *would* be. I kept hoping I'd wake up to my parents comforting me with a smile explaining that we all have nightmares from time to time. Instead, I was stuck with the cruel reality that everything we owned was burning a few feet away, even the Christmas presents we'd just opened a few days earlier. It was all up in flames.

I cried out, asking to go back and get my dolls, but my mother just hugged me tighter. We cried out for Princess, hoping she'd come running toward us before we left. Surely she had escaped and was hiding somewhere safe. The thought of her being left inside our burning home tormented me.

Soon I realized the car wasn't moving and Daddy and Reagan were inside the garage. Daddy yelled to Reagan, "Put it in neutral!" Since Mom's car keys were in the house, Daddy pushed her car out of the garage with Reagan's help, keeping it from burning like everything else. We were all yelling for them to hurry. I was terrified the garage would collapse with them inside. Everything was out of control. I was about to lose more than just my house!

Daddy jumped in the driver's seat of the Buick while Reagan hopped in the front seat. We finally were all together and safe. My brother was only fourteen, but that night he was Daddy's right-hand man, and he was no disappointment.

Daddy drove us safely toward the highway, never looking back as the rest of us turned and saw our home burning to the ground. The car was filled with the sound of our sobs, but suddenly there was silence. It was as if we'd all realized at the same time it *wasn't* a nightmare. This was real life. One breath in. One breath out.

I was so grateful for my father. He was the sweetest hero in the world. He drove us to Rob and Betty Billingsly's house, our close neighbors, and kept us all as calm as possible.

When he banged on their door, Mr. Billingsly opened it. Daddy yelled inside, "Call the fire department! Our house is on fire!"

We jumped out of the car and ran into the safety of their house, while Mr. Billingsly followed Daddy back to the fire. To our surprise, several men were gathered in the kitchen eating breakfast before a fishing trip.

One of the men there was my close friend Pam's dad, Frank Edmond. Pam and I often played together and went to the same church, so her dad was no stranger. He hugged me and held me tight, assuring me it would be okay. He did not want to let go. It made me feel safe.

From the large kitchen window, we could see the fire raging. We gathered around and watched our house burn. I sobbed into my mother's arms, "My play kitchen and Betsy Wetsy doll are burning!"

Caitlin called out, "We have to find Princess!"

Mrs. Billingsly rushed around the house gathering blankets, socks, and a robe for my mother. The adults in the room were trying to stay calm, yet I heard their voices quiver. Tears rolled down my mom's cheeks. She tried to stay strong for us kids, but eventually it became too much, and she cried without control. I knew she was afraid too. We all were.

I sat near the kitchen sink rubbing my cold feet, watching the fire erupt and consume more of our house. Finally, we heard the sirens, and the fire trucks arrive.

Mr. Edmond put his hand on my shoulder and asked, "Do you want to go home with me? We can go wake Pam and y'all can play."

I liked the idea. Playing with Pam would make everything okay. After all, wasn't this just a bad dream? He took me to his house and woke the family. Soon Pam, her brother Bobby, and mother Karen walked sleepily down the hall toward me. Mr. Edmond explained calmly that my house was on fire.

In that surreal moment, as I explained to Pam what had happened, it felt like I was talking about a stranger's house. My numbness continued throughout the next day. I walked around Pam's house robotically repeating, "My house burned down. My house burned down."

I was grateful to have this special family love me and make this devastating day more bearable. Pam gave me some of her pretty clothes and favorite toys. I didn't want to seem ungrateful, but I silently wanted my own things. I wanted Princess back, but sadly she hadn't returned and was never found, adding to our sorrows.

Later that afternoon we drove out to what was left of my house. Smoldering ashes greeted us, adding to the finality of the moment. Cars were parked on the side of the road watching the smoke rise from a distance. I later learned that the firefighters had to make over forty trips to town throughout the day to fill up with water because the pipes were frozen around our house due to the recent snowstorm.

Mom and some of her closest friends were walking through the ashes as they picked up the remains of a few cherished keepsakes blackened and charred. The brick fireplace was the only thing left standing. Pam and I watched in disbelief. Through tears she hugged me and then walked to her mother's car and returned with her doll Molly. "I love Molly, and I love you. I want you to have her." We both cried as I held her well-loved doll tightly, knowing it was her favorite. That doll remained a precious treasure, just as our friendship had been a treasure to me. A few years later she moved away, but our close friendship continued.

Chapter 2

A CHILDHOOD FRIENDSHIP

My childhood was surrounded by love as our community of Guthrie, Oklahoma and loving church family helped us get back on our feet. They replaced all the Christmas presents that Reagan, Caitlin, and I had gotten but were burned in the fire. They threw parties for us and showered us with love. The insurance helped rebuild our home, and soon an almost normal life returned. It took years, however, before I could relax and enjoy a fire in the fireplace. Some days I wondered if I would ever feel safe again. Nightmares would pop into my world unexpectedly, with vivid, dangerous flames of fire running toward me.

My life wasn't perfect, but I knew that I was more fortunate than most, living in a newly rebuilt home, with Christian parents who took me to church regularly, and caring grandparents who also loved the Lord. To the east of us was a field of beautiful grass, crepe myrtles, and bald cypress trees that became my dream playground and prayer garden.

I was younger than most of my friends when I knew in my heart that I wanted Jesus as my Lord and Savior. I knelt by my bed and prayed often, knowing Jesus was happy to assure me He was there for me. Ever since I was baptized, I have truly felt as though I have never been alone. How thankful I am for that special relationship I've enjoyed basically my entire life. Despite my troubles, God was good; God is good—all the time.

In the summer of 1976, Pam and I were in high school. Frank,

Karen, Pam, and her brother Bobby had moved years ago to Edmond, Oklahoma, just a small distance from Guthrie. I am grateful our parents encouraged our friendship to grow and allowed us to visit each other frequently.

One of our favorite things to do when I was visiting her was to ride our bikes down the street to visit her aunt, June Walker. That short, stocky lady always smiled and treated me like a queen. She loved to laugh and feed anyone who walked into her house. Laughter and food were simply gifts she enjoyed sharing with others.

June's youngest son popped in surprisingly one afternoon. For years, I'd heard about the family favorite, Jackson Bruce Walker, but his busy schedule kept our paths from crossing, until that Saturday afternoon. I'd heard many entertaining stories and seen several pictures of handsome J.B., or Bruce, as most people referred to him. Pam's eyes lit up every time she talked about her cousin Bruce. He was four years older than we were and was quite a celebrity in their family.

That Saturday, Bruce turned into the driveway in his red sports car, dressed in white tennis attire, his black curls wet from exertion. He stopped just long enough to give his mom a huge bear hug and to grab a handful of pretzels from the crystal bowl sitting on the coffee table. It took me a minute to realize he was "the Jackson Bruce Walker" I'd heard so much about.

My heart skipped a beat as he approached me and Pam in the living room. I was utterly taken by his adorable grin that made him look just like the sweet boy next door. I would later find out he was anything but sweet. I could feel the heat in my face as I'm sure I blushed. Bruce breezed through the house to his room, where he showered and later left to meet friends. Every time after that, my heart sped up when I saw Jackson Bruce Walker.

Chapter 3

HEALTH ISSUES

OTHERS HAVE DESCRIBED ME as a people person who had an easy smile from ear to ear, on the days I felt well. I'd developed some stomach issues in my late twenties, and they were becoming more concerning, but I certainly tried to be positive and pleasant. Day after day I would keep a journal of what food I had, thinking I had an allergy. Every time I ate, I had severe symptoms. I thought getting allergy-tested would reveal the problem. It was yet another doctor to call and get an appointment scheduled. How many doctors had I already seen? I was consumed with being my own self-advocate while feeling weak and discouraged.

Unfortunately, the allergy test came back weeks later with no answers. My condition was not due to a food allergy. I left my doctor's office extremely frustrated. My health was declining, and I was getting absolutely no answers from the slew of doctors I'd already seen. Friends and family started to look at me with concern, realizing I was dropping weight quickly and my eyes were beginning to look sunken.

The numerous gastroenterologists I saw would just tell me I had irritable bowel syndrome (IBS) and give me another prescription. Five years prior, my stomach started bloating daily to a point where I only wore elastic pants and blousy tops to camouflage my belly. One lady even asked me when my baby was due! No one gave me any real medical relief, even after seeing various specialists in the area.

I *kept* losing weight, and if I ate anything at all, even a bite of toast or cheese, I bloated throughout the day. As a result, I would only eat right before I went to bed. I was accustomed to being hungry most of the time, but I knew what would happen almost immediately if I ate. The swelling and tiredness were not worth a few bites of food. All day I would look forward to the hour before bedtime when I could gorge myself with food while Lauren, my precious daughter, was asleep, knowing I would bloat, go to sleep on my stomach, and hope that the swelling was down the next morning. Being divorced and being a single mom with severe health issues had never been part of my plan.

Chapter 4

GETTING REACQUAINTED

2000

Twenty-plus years later I was reacquainted with Bruce Walker. We had both experienced marriages and divorces during that time, and I was in my late thirties when our paths crossed again. One day when my daughter Lauren and I were at the grocery store, we ran into Pam's Aunt June. When she saw me, she quickly sprinted to my cart with a grin. Her short stature, beautiful smile, and grayish-brown curls reminded me of the lady I loved when I was in high school.

"Look at you, little lady!" June oohed and awed over my sweet Lauren. "You both need to come over sometime when Bruce is there."

Obviously, June was playing matchmaker. My heart fluttered at the thought of Bruce's dark curls and flirtatious grin the last time I'd seen him in his living room.

"You know, Bruce is always helping out the homeless on holidays." June pressed her lips together and smiled. "If you ever need a chaperone to a Sunday school function, Bruce would be great company."

He still seemed like that good, all-American guy I remembered when we were teenagers. My life had changed in the decades since I had last seen Bruce. I was no longer the tall brunette with hair down to my waist. It was chopped off at the shoulders for low maintenance purposes, but it was perfect for my age. A tad of gray hair was beginning to peek in places, a little earlier than I had hoped, but not enough for me to cringe yet.

A quarter of a century is a long time to be apart, and my life circumstances had changed too. I was a single mom with health problems and had a teenage daughter who was the light of my entire world. I had no interest in getting involved with anyone. I believe that is what made my friendship with Bruce unique and genuine once we finally decided to spend time together.

Bruce Friendship

As time passed, Bruce became a sweet listener and an advocate for me. His sea-blue eyes were mesmerizing as he listened to me describe every ache and pain I felt. He was consistently researching places I could find medical answers within the area and elsewhere. How blessed I was to have him in my life after all these years.

When I called him a few days after seeing one of my many doctors, he asked, "Becca, do you want to come over and talk?"

I took him up on the offer and drove straight to his house. What I saw shocked and confused me. A yard sale and a FOR SALE sign were prominently staked in Bruce's lawn. I was on the verge of losing my composure but managed to control my emotions. He never mentioned he was leaving. I knew we did not talk daily, but I thought he would tell me if he was moving.

As I walked into his house, I was pleasantly surprised to see his mother's smiling face. June still looked much like she used to, but the sound of her oxygen machine let me know right away the years had crept up on her. She was busy packing, so I sat near her, helping with the crystal and china from Bruce's hutch.

I couldn't help but reach out for her hand. "I remember when I was in your home long ago. Each time Pam and I would stop over, you always made me feel special."

June's eyes teared up and she grabbed both of my hands as she softly said, "It sure has made me happy to see you and Bruce spending time together. I've always thought you were extra special."

I hated to disappoint her, but I knew I would not be dating material with my health issues. Sharing my frustration about my health openly with her seemed to be the right thing to do. I certainly did not want her thinking that Bruce and I had a relationship that would be anything other than a friendship, yet one that I valued. There had never been any flirtation between us. Our relationship was more like brother and sister, or good friends.

I finally got up the courage to ask Bruce, "Why are you moving? You never mentioned it before."

He answered with an easy smile, "I'm not sure what direction I'm taking next in my life. I might keep traveling with my business, or maybe stay closer to home." He glanced at his mother, making me believe he might stay close by to care for her.

I nodded. "Where are you going to move?"

"I'm not sure. I might rent something until I figure things out. I found a duplex close to your house."

I was surprised, but excited. The thought of this kind, thoughtful man living near me was a comfort. He called me later that night, thrilled to tell me that he sold his house the first day it was on the market!

Soon, Bruce had moved within walking distance from the house where my daughter and I lived. Our house was not fancy, but it was ours. We knew most of the neighbors and felt blessed to be living close to people who wanted to help us in any way. I had always been told that it takes a village to raise a child. As a single mom, I needed support. My neighbors and friends came to my rescue many times and felt like my village.

Bruce knew that I was sick, and my work requirements were causing me to feel a great deal of pressure. I'd recently accepted a new position as the hospital's department chair for the social workers, which carried additional responsibilities. He surprised me as we sat in my small, simply furnished living room talking about the frustrations I was feeling.

He surprised me one day, making me feel like we'd become much closer than perhaps I'd realized. He took my hand and said, "I have arranged for you to have a condo any weekend you choose next month."

We discussed and debated, but he would not take no for an answer.

Bruce did not make a big deal out of it. "I'm just helping out a friend," he said. He never wanted to bring attention to himself, which was one of the many qualities I admired in him. He was an extremely humble and kind listener. I could not help but think that he still had that same high school smile, pretty head of hair, and charm, and yet the years had created some thinning. His black curls now had a few silver streaks, which made him look distinguished.

I was about to give him a big hug and thank him for his thoughtful offer, but he glanced at his phone, realizing he had to get back to work. The door opened and shut without an opportunity to even voice my appreciation. He was that kind of genuine and selfless person. Soon after, Lauren and I enjoyed a stress-free weekend trip a few hours away, just the two of us. I appreciated the unexpected and generous gift.

Bruce would pop over with a bouquet of flowers and a smile from time to time. He was busy running his own computer business and was devoted to taking care of his elderly mother. Consequently, we did not talk every day. He attended a men's in-depth Bible study weekly, which required him to read and study quite a bit. We rarely ate together, but when we did, he knew to expect me to feel uncomfortable and to shorten our visit.

One Friday night he asked, "Don't you want to eat something, anything at all?"

Embarrassed, I looked away, saying, "You really don't want to hear a lady burp for hours, do you?"

Bruce laughed loudly, reminding me of Daddy's laughs that

could be heard almost next door, and said, "Sure I do! We can burp together. Let's have a burping contest."

Lying on the sofa after eating two pieces of pizza, I burped the entire time it took for us to watch a movie. I'm not sure who burped or laughed the loudest, but tears of happiness rolled down my cheeks. Bruce was truly a blessing in my life. Who else would encourage me to eat, burp, and then turn the embarrassment into laughter? I couldn't thank him enough for coming back into my life.

Trip with Our Mothers (2001)

Several months later, Bruce and his mother invited me and my mother on a short road trip. Going out of town sounded like a fun change of pace. Our mothers talked and laughed in the back seat as though they had known each other for years. They giggled like sisters. We had a wonderful three-day getaway, talking and laughing nonstop.

During the trip we met his oldest brother, Mike, and his wife, Kay, who welcomed us with open arms into their beautifully decorated home, serving an elaborate meal for us. I hoped they were not offended when I ate sparingly to prevent my discomfort. They were outgoing and personable with the gift of hospitality. Bruce's mother kept smiling and patting my hand. I knew she was hoping my friendship with Bruce would grow into something even more. I was certain that my mother shared those same wishes. When we returned home, I unpacked my suitcase, and I couldn't help but think how comfortable I was with Bruce and his family.

I caught myself daydreaming, seeing a beautiful life unfold with him, when I told myself aloud, "I am in no shape for this! Quit daydreaming!"

I knew I did not have much to offer anyone. I certainly did not feel attractive, and my health issues remained a mystery. How attractive was my endless burping? I did not feel well enough physically to do much. Most of my friends were meeting at restaurants, at each other's houses, or going to events in the community. Since I was having so many digestive issues, I could not eat much. I knew it made my friends uncomfortable to eat in front of me. As a result, I started staying home more and more.

Bruce kept me company even though I did very little that others would think was exciting. We shared our favorite Bible verses, talked openly from the heart, laughed, cried, and sat in my backyard and talked about everything and nothing all at the same time.

I'd witnessed his attentive caretaking many times when he was with his mother, whether he was at her luxury apartment, his place, or on the road. The oxygen machine might beep one time before he quickly adjusted it. He created a medication checklist for his mom to use when she took each pill. Not all sons were that attentive and supportive of their mothers' needs. Bruce did the same for me, often sharing medical facilities he had researched and possible answers to my medical problems. He was diligent in researching my symptoms. I couldn't help but think how unique Bruce was. He was almost too perfect to be real.

Chapter 5

A LAST RESORT - 2001

Trip to Johns Hopkins Medical Center

You don't realize how much people celebrate and mourn with food until you can't eat. Food is the center of every gathering. Meals increasingly became difficult for me because everything I ate caused me pain. As a result, my social circles diminished, changing my otherwise outgoing nature to survival mode as a near recluse. My world was shrinking.

Even after taking communion, the swelling process would start. So I stopped taking it. One day while talking to my minister and his wife, I cried as I explained how much I missed taking communion. My minister was so thoughtful and offered to take communion for me, which he did many times thereafter. Communion was something I enjoyed, but I must admit I took it for granted. We all take things for granted until they are taken from us.

Over the years I'd exhausted the list of local gastroenterologists and had grown discouraged. My low weight was becoming a concern, and my appearance had changed dramatically. The mirror showed hollow cheeks and dark circles under my eyes. I was not getting stronger, and I certainly wasn't getting answers to my health issues.

My precious and loving mother knew I needed medical answers, and quickly. Mom was so strong until the weight of my declining health took its toll on her. She seemed to age rapidly as my medical issues progressed.

We gathered all my medical reports, packed a few bags, and

flew across the country to the Johns Hopkins Medical Center in Baltimore, Maryland, without an appointment. This was our last resort. They had an exceptional reputation, but unfortunately the waiting list was three months long and that was too long to wait.

Three large notebooks of medical records weighed me down as we got on the plane. Mom offered to help carry one of them, but her hands were noticeably shaking and I didn't have the heart to share my burden. She knew this might be our last chance to save my life.

We didn't talk much on that flight. We were both so afraid but dared not speak words of fear. How I yearned for Daddy, our hero, to be sitting next to us to bring us strength. Daddy was suddenly taken from us over a decade ago from a massive heart attack.

Once our plane landed, we dropped off our luggage at the hotel and called a cab to take us to McDonald's, knowing very well what would happen next. That Sunday afternoon, I devoured an entire hamburger, swelled as usual, and went to the emergency room connected to the medical center, praying this was our entrance to the healthcare I so desperately needed.

The ER doctor examined me, then measured my abdomen repeatedly. His eyes were wide with surprise as he recorded the measurements while listening to me burp nonstop. I shared the medical reports I had brought spanning the past seven years and answered all his questions.

I'll never forget the fear in my mother's voice as she explained the situation. "Doctor, we have come across the country without an appointment. We were told the waiting list is three months long, but we don't have that kind of time. I'm afraid. You see, she has a daughter to raise. Please tell me you will help us."

My life was in the doctor's hands. If he decided not to treat me, our gamble would be lost.

Brows furrowed, he told us, "Be at the gastrointestinal clinic tomorrow morning at 9:00 a.m. I'm scheduling you right away."

"God, thank you!" I shouted and then cried in relief.

Mom hugged me and we both thanked Dr. Harrison repeatedly. Finally, we would get the answers for which we'd been searching.

The next three weeks were filled with doctor appointments, tests, and brief respites in the rooftop swimming pool at the hotel as we waited for answers. Mom watched me swim, trying to encourage me daily, but my belly continued to be extended. I ate very little, and I noticed Mom was choosing not to eat much in front of me, even when I begged her. I'm not sure who was hurting the most—mother for daughter or daughter for mother.

When we finally met with the team of doctors, they informed us the battery of tests I'd endured over three weeks had not brought the answers we'd prayed about. The best doctors in the country had no more answers than our local physicians. I remember thinking: How can I return home to my daughter without answers? Will I survive long enough to watch her graduate from high school? Will I ever find relief from the constant pain and worry?

The lead gastroenterologist took a step forward, almost hesitantly. "There is one last test we can perform, but we won't be able to schedule it until next week."

I replied, "I have no choice, doctor. This is our last resort!"

Disappointed to not have answers, and desperately missing my daughter, I called Lauren and told her the news. She had watched me suffer over the past seven years and had missed so much in her young life because of my illness. Guilt and pride tore through me as Lauren excitedly told me she'd been voted into the homecoming court. We both cried as she begged me to come home to help her pick out a dress and shoes. It broke my heart that I might miss such an important event in her life. I wanted to promise her I would be there on time, but this was out of my control.

We were blessed with wonderful friends who could take her shopping, but I was heartsick about not being there for her. I missed her desperately but knew this last test at Johns Hopkins could be key to fixing my broken body and allow me to have the normal life we'd both so desperately wanted. Lauren wanted me today, but I had to think past tomorrow.

The following week I endured the most painful experience of my life. The procedure lasted eight hours and was much more painful than childbirth. God was with me, helping me get through the nightmarish experience. It was excruciating, and I am not sure I could go through it again to save my life. Thankfully, I had not spent the week before worrying about it, unaware of how painful it would be.

In preparation for the test, six people held me down on the hospital bed as they pushed tubes up into my body without any pain medication. In intervals, they would ask me to eat or drink while they watched what happened inside of me on a motility screen, much like an EKG screen.

To everyone's surprise, my colon showed no signs of movement and remained flatlined, even after a surge of motility medicine. Every doctor and nurse looked bewildered. This was not something they'd seen often.

After four exceedingly long weeks in Maryland, I had a diagnosis: my colon was totally paralyzed. I was both relieved and in shock. I had so many questions for the doctors. Was this a progressive disease? What would this mean for the quality of my life? Would it affect my other organs? What now? I still had more questions than answers, even after waiting seven years for the diagnosis.

Chapter 6

THE NEXT STEP

ILEOSTOMY (2002)

We flew home with motility drugs prescribed and prayed for a miracle. Returning to my normal life left me in survival mode. Work requirements, Lauren's afterschool activities, and life in general were more than I could manage on most days.

I was grateful Mom was able to stay with us often. We both thanked God for her support and love. It took a toll on her though. I saw the concern and worry on her face as she watched me go through the motions. Overwhelming sadness engulfed me for both my mother and daughter as they suffered along with me. It was more than I thought I could endure.

The motility medicine didn't seem to help one bit, and I was instructed to increase the dose each week, hoping for a miracle. It made me feel groggy, but my bloating continued. Unfortunately, my body was unresponsive to the treatment. Months later, I finally agreed to an ileostomy, where they surgically sewed the end of my small intestines onto the surface of the skin. The waste would pass out of the ileostomy into a bag. It was my last option. Prayerfully I asked God to allow the surgery to bypass my inactive colon and allow me to eat more often and help me gain strength.

Mom, my sister Caitlin, and I caught an early Sunday morning flight across the country back to the Johns Hopkins facility. Caitlin joined us on this trip, and it thrilled me and Mom both to have her company. More importantly, Mom needed her emotional support. The ileostomy surgery was performed on Tuesday. When I woke,

I saw the bag and my ileostomy stoma, the opening of the colon, for the first time. I turned away. It was difficult to look at, but the nurse was there to instruct me on how to keep it clean. I gagged, not believing that my body changed so drastically. Mom cleaned the stoma until I could handle it myself without heaving. Jesus and my mother were by my side.

I was not emotionally prepared for how much my life would change with the ileostomy bag. I now had to choose clothing to hide it, especially if it was filling up with waste. The bag would fill with air, much like a large balloon, and I needed to make frequent trips to the bathroom to release it. It became a priority to leave the house with extra supplies and a change of clothing. I lived in constant dread that the ileostomy bag would pop like a balloon from the pressure and contents would run down my leg, especially when I was at work. It was a daily emotional struggle. People I'd talked to with ileostomies had not experienced these same issues. I worried that my small intestine was becoming paralyzed too.

Nearby communities were praying for me. I received letters with prayers and encouraging notes from nearby churches with signatures of people I didn't even know. I had never experienced this before. It was humbling. Praying for other people was something I loved doing and had done most of my life, but I had never known what it was like for a group of people to gather and pray for me. Honestly, there were days when I did not feel like praying, yet these people filled the gap.

I managed. That was about it. I worked, drove Lauren to her afterschool activities when I could, and went to church, but declined to do much socially for the next few years. Bruce was consistently patient with me as he ran errands, watched movies with me, and checked on us daily.

Fell in Love with Bruce

Over this two-year period, in my simply landscaped backyard, I fell in love unexpectedly with Bruce. He became my best friend and seemed to understand my medical discomfort.

Bruce held my hand for the first time on the afternoon of May 21, 2003. That day I knew if he ever asked me, I would happily marry him. I felt safe with him, and my sweet memories from when I was a little girl added to my affection for him. Like Bruce, his family and especially his cousin Pam were easy to love. I don't remember any time in my life without Pam.

Bruce's parents had always reminded me of my own parents, warm, welcoming, and genuine people who made me feel accepted and valued. His mother June would always ask me how things were going, but she looked me in the eye and listened to my response as if I were the only one in the room. She always acted as if she had nothing more important to do than to give me her undivided attention. His dad, Robby, whom I'd known as a child, had a deep voice and jolly chuckle that warmed my heart each time he gave me a big bear hug. Unfortunately, he passed away unexpectedly from an aneurysm when Bruce was in his twenties.

Bruce had never been a father, but he was good to Lauren. They quickly grew fond of each other and loved spending time together. He was a good listener, appearing kind and caring.

I was most thankful for our spiritual relationship because I felt most men would not have seen me as attractive with my physical issues. He appeared so godly that he reminded me that our relationship was blessed by Jesus and was much more than what most passionate relationships were. We prayed often and shared Bible verses we both loved. His Bible was tabbed, written in often, highlighted, and worn. It was obvious that he carried it almost everywhere. This meant everything to me because I would only consider spending quality time with a man who had a relationship with God.

Chapter 7

OUR ENGAGEMENT

JANUARY 1, 2004

New Year's Eve we danced the night away. My heart was racing, and my feet were screaming for a rest, but every dance with Bruce made time stand still. The elegant event center was warm and welcoming. Beautiful mahogany walls, crystal chandeliers, and an enlarged dance floor set the mood. Waiters and waitresses were at our beck and call.

When midnight came, the man of my dreams led me to our table. My heart was beating fast, and my feet were hurting from the night of dancing, but when Bruce knelt beside the table and pulled an ornate key with gold fringe from his pocket, I knew something very special was happening. Time stood still. I did not see faces or hear music. It was as if Bruce and I were all alone in the room, although there were hundreds of strangers surrounding us. I felt the peace, the quiet, the stillness in the moment.

My heart sparked with love as Bruce looked at me with dashing blue eyes and knelt to propose. We both shed tears of joy when Bruce placed a key in my hand. He reached in his pocket and pulled out a piece of paper and read me this note:

Dearest Becca,

The key that I am giving you tonight is a symbol of many things:

You are the key to my happiness.

You alone hold the key to my heart.

You have unlocked the door to my heart and ignited it with love.

Our love for each other is a miracle blessed by God.

Our love is an everlasting love.

You are the key to my happiness and an answer to my prayers.

This key represents Jesus, the key to our future filled with faith, love, caring, joy, passion, honor, and friendship.

I love you, Becca, and want you as my wife. With God's help we will have a blessed and fulfilled life. We will do wonderful things together.

Let's always remember that the key to each other is Jesus.

He concluded by quoting scripture:

"Now we see but a poor reflection as in a mirror; then we shall see face to face. Now I know in part; then I shall know fully, even as I am fully known. And now these three remain: faith, hope, and love; but the greatest of these is love" (1 Corinthians 13:12-13 CSB).

When he stopped, I knew Bruce was my forever love. We both cried as we embraced. My head was spinning as I realized my new life was about to begin.

Unfortunately, the key would be an important symbol for the insidious lock with which Bruce would bind my life for years to come.

When we told my sweet daughter our plans the next morning, her smile was pasted from ear to ear. For the next month, her golden ponytail swung back and forth, and her walk was more like a skip. The excitement, joy, and love that we felt from our families were more than a celebration.

Bruce's mother, June, was overjoyed to hear the news. She said it was the best New Year's she could remember. We had no idea at the time it would be her last. She told me in confidence that she'd always thought Bruce and I were meant for each other, then folded me in an embrace, whispering I was an answer to her prayers. It wasn't until twenty-one months later I understood why she had been praying for him.

My mother was giddy with a smile that was larger than life! Mom had worried about my health for years, but now I had someone devoted to me who could help take care of me.

Bruce's Mother Died

Five weeks later Bruce and I rushed his mom to the hospital. Her health had declined the last few months before our engagement, and COPD made it difficult for her to do much more than rest in bed. Although I knew she struggled, I had no idea how ill she was.

The last words I spoke to her in the hospital were, "Don't worry about Bruce. I promise I will take care of him."

She closed her eyes and breathed her last breath. I meant every word, and it made me feel better that she knew I'd be there to watch over her son.

The next few days sped by quickly as preparations were made for her funeral. The church was packed with Bruce's relatives, many of whom I had never met. The crowd was massive, making it obvious June was loved and respected by others, too many to count. Thankfully, Lauren and I were able to meet several of them, and they treated us like they had known us all our lives.

Days after the funeral, Bruce and his two older brothers, Mike and Doug, divided her possessions. When Bruce invited me to his mother's home, he showed me what he had chosen. Beaming with pride once again, I just sat back and smiled at the man I was going to marry. He chose a wedding picture of his mother and various sentimental things rather than furs, large pieces of furniture, and crystal. His actions came as no shock to me; they were quite revealing of his character, or at least, the persona he wished for me to perceive.

Bruce was amazing under pressure. He remained calm even after burying his mother, taking care of her estate, and the pressures of keeping up with traveling for work. He was dedicated to our relationship. By all outward appearances he had a gift to juggle many responsibilities under the worst of circumstances.

When he asked me if I would like to move the wedding up from the summer to March or April, it lit a fire under me. Lauren and I were thrilled as we started talking about our future.

We decided to sell my house on Summit Avenue and temporarily rent while we looked for a new house, either to buy or build something the three of us could design. Bruce really liked the idea of building a house, thinking it would be a fun project in which we could include Lauren. All he had to do was tell his leasing agent he would need to break his lease, then he would be free to move.

A few weeks before the wedding, I panicked. I'd ask him questions like, "What if you get sick at the sight of my ileostomy bag? I wouldn't blame you. Don't you even want to see it before we get married? What about the swelling and my burping? Even though things have improved, I am far from perfect."

Bruce smiled the sweetest smile and reassured me. "Becca, I love you for you, no matter what. I've seen pictures of ileostomy bags and how to care for them. That doesn't faze me in the least. Besides, I have witnessed your swelling, and we have laughed and burped together many times. You have nothing to worry about."

I never dreamed anyone could be so incredible to me. I also never dreamed the nightmare that awaited me by marrying this man I thought I knew.

A few days later, Bruce came over to my house to help me prepare for a garage sale as we prepared for the move. I surprised him when I walked into the room as he was working on my computer. Looking back, I realize he was hiding something when he quickly blackened my computer screen. At the time I had no reason to be suspicious.

Bruce said, "Becca, my dad would be proud of you. It doesn't take much to make you happy. In fact, we've fallen in love sitting in your backyard. That is why I feel comfortable showing you something. Before I do, I want us to agree to never touch it until we are old and gray. Agree?"

What was I supposed to say? At the time I had no idea what

he was referring to, as he'd never talked like this before. When the screen appeared, it showed a portfolio of close to a million dollars.

I looked at Bruce in disbelief. When he explained what I was looking at, I said, "My dad would be proud of you. He always believed in living beneath your means, and you do just that very thing."

I hugged him and felt relieved that money wouldn't be an issue. I was overwhelmed with gratitude. "You cut coupons and look for a bargain, and you don't even have to."

In that moment, I felt as certain as I had about anything in my life. Bruce admired me for being down-to-earth and non-materialistic, and I admired him for being humble and conservative.

He explained his computer business averaged a $200,000 balance, but at times it dwindled pretty low, depending on the need to order merchandise for his clients. We agreed to stick to a budget and to keep our jobs. God was blessing us with a bright future.

Chapter 8

THE ALMOST PERFECT DAY

THE WEDDING

We married on a beautiful April morning. Bruce reserved a limousine to take Mom, Lauren, and me to the church. It was just one of many gestures he made to show his love, a love for which I had always hoped. Bruce requested the driver take the scenic route to the church. It was absolutely beautiful with waterfalls and rock formations on both sides of the road. Oklahoma had always been my home, and its beauty never was a disappointment.

As we entered the intimate chapel, most everyone was there except Bruce's oldest brother Mike and his wife Kay. We waited, called them, then finally saw them walk in the door. They were frazzled and nothing like I'd remembered during our road trip to see them with our mothers in tow. We could tell something was wrong, something was terribly wrong, yet our minister, family, and friends were all seated and smiling. The soft music started, indicating the ceremony was about to begin.

It was a simple wedding with only a few flowers, immediate family, and close friends. Our minister, Reverend Stallings, opened the service with these words:

"It brings me great pleasure to be a part of today. Bruce and Becca have an amazing relationship based on their faith in God. During our premarital counseling sessions, they took a personality and compatibility test that scored the highest that was possible. Their faith, their compatibility scores, their intertwined family history, and those of you who are here today make this a glorious day to celebrate!"

The love I saw in Bruce's sea-blue eyes was a gift any woman would dream about. His smile made this the happiest day of my life. The only thing that did not make this day perfect was the expression on my now sister-in-law's face. It was obvious Kay was not herself. Something was bothering her greatly, and I wondered if it had something to do with their late arrival at our service. Later, when I asked her about it, she said she'd been suffering from a migraine. Certainly, wouldn't anyone be frazzled with a migraine? Wouldn't they? Yet something didn't seem right. But it wasn't my place to pry.

After the ceremony, Bruce's Aunt Karen hosted a lovely wedding reception at her house with help from her daughter, Pam. They'd put a lot of thought into every detail, which made it really special for us. Bruce had become almost a second son to Karen, especially after her son Bobby, Pam's brother, had been tragically killed in a car wreck several years before. Pam gave a beautiful toast asking God to bless our marriage. We had pictures taken, and we all sat down for a wonderful meal, and afterward we thanked everyone for joining us on our special day.

The last thing I remember was hugging my precious Lauren. Her long golden curls and bright smile lit up the room. Over the past seven years, she'd endured a great deal of pain with my health problems. Bruce had given her a chapter of joy in her life that helped her believe the future would be full of many blessings.

At the end of the night, the limousine was waiting for us. We waved to the wedding party and blew kisses as we drove off to catch our honeymoon flight to the beach.

My mind flashed to the day I'd met Bruce in high school. It was amazing to now see him wearing the wedding ring I'd placed on his finger hours earlier. We were husband and wife! I was actually married to "the Jackson Bruce Walker" and I could not have been happier.

Chapter 9

AN ALMOST PERFECT HONEYMOON

BRUCE WAS A PLANNER by nature and had thought through literally every detail of our honeymoon. I learned the truth of that statement later. Because he knew I loved the water, he planned a trip to the beach. Every day was wonderful in almost every way. Even the weather cooperated.

Two surprises stand out, among all the fun activities Bruce planned for us. First was the surprise parasailing trip where he was exceptionally thoughtful. He asked the man working in the boat to tell me in detail what he was doing so I would feel safe. Not every husband was as caring as Bruce.

The second surprise was the day he rented a pristine blue convertible. It was a picture-perfect day full of smiles, laughter, holding hands, and sightseeing. We blazed a trail down the road as I beamed brightly, wearing a big floppy hat. His silvery black curls, flying in the wind, made me think back to our childhood. We laughed and acted like teenagers, footloose and fancy-free! Every day he told me, "I just want to keep that smile on your face forever."

It was a relaxing trip for me, but unfortunately, Bruce had to work several hours every day. The computer networking business was demanding and time-consuming. He used the lobby's guest computer to follow up with clients and check emails but was apologetic and assured me he would work as quickly as possible.

I was still eating just a little each day, trying to minimize my digestive issues. Even though Bruce had been extremely supportive during the years, my goal was to keep the symptoms to a minimum during our honeymoon. Bruce was again exceptionally thoughtful, not putting an emphasis on fancy restaurants and meals. Out of respect, he ate mainly when he was working in the lobby.

During those afternoons, I swam in the luxurious hotel pool, read a romance novel, and napped while he worked. I felt like a queen being pampered and blessed beyond measure.

My honeymoon was almost perfect if I overlooked the hours he spent working, and the fact that we did not spend time together over meals. My health issues were in the forefront of my mind. I tried to focus on the good things, but I still felt a little slighted by his inability to set aside his work for a few days as we celebrated our union.

Chapter 10

OUR NEW LIFE TOGETHER

WHEN BRUCE AND I married, I already had an ileostomy, but my physical symptoms of bloating and discomfort continued. We were always searching for answers and ideas that could help me recover completely. Bruce continued to be amazing at researching new treatments and the best places we could go to seek answers. Even though he would often go out of town for his job, he always came back with the same concern about my health.

I could not have asked for a more comforting, compassionate, and knowledgeable advocate than my husband. He was an answer to my prayers. Every morning and night he would bring my medicine like clockwork. He seemed to be a natural caretaker, just like he'd been for his mother.

Moved to Ivy Avenue House

Soon after we married, I sold my house and many of my belongings. It was sad to walk away from the place Lauren and I called home for twelve years, the home we'd loved. But our future with Bruce was exciting and gave me hope for the years to come.

Life had not been easy for us in the past, but I'd taken care of Lauren despite my health issues and I'd managed financially. It wasn't always easy paying for my medical bills, the mortgage, and all the other bills while pursuing a master's degree as a single mother. I felt a sense of pride in this accomplishment but also knew God had helped me every step of the way. I deposited the proceeds from the sale of my house in my personal account, feeling thankful, looking forward to finding a new place to live.

The search took a turn I'd not expected. Every house we looked at Bruce would find something he did not like about it. He was normally a positive person, but somehow, he couldn't help but say things like, "There aren't enough windows. We will want more storage. This house doesn't have a large enough yard." It was clear he wanted to build our home. Reluctantly, I agreed.

We put several of my things in storage and moved into our Ivy Avenue rental house while we built our dream home. He wanted a pool and pool house, which seemed extravagant to me.

When I would question him about these things, he would kindly say, "We are going to dedicate this home to the Lord. We're going to host Bible studies, youth groups, and retreats for the glory of God. The pool and pool house will be just the icing on the cake for these events." And later he'd say, "Besides, Becca, I know how much you love to swim. This would make my mother happy knowing we are together at last and building a future together."

It was overwhelming. But Bruce assured me he would take the lead and not bother me with details so I could focus on my daughter, my health, and my work. All my single friends would say, "Pray for me to meet someone just like Bruce!"

I continued to watch the relationship between Lauren and Bruce grow stronger. She was close to her biological father, Scott, but he lived out of town, so they did not get to see each other on a weekly basis. We divorced when Lauren was young, but always co-parented in a positive way. Bruce had a gift of relating to young people. It was like he had been a part of our lives all along, and he was comfortable being both a friend and a father figure in her life. Lauren beamed with pride when friends would come around to meet him.

My mom loved Bruce and was ecstatic that we were married and were making plans for our future. She had tried to stay strong after my dad died and my digestive issues erupted. She had given up so much of her life to take care of Lauren and me. After my dad and both of her parents had passed away, it was time for her to enjoy some things she wanted and desired, yet she was driven to help me in any way.

As you can imagine, when Bruce won my heart, he also won my mother's. She had her dream of me being loved again and taken care of, while giving her a new lease on life with the freedom to spend time with friends and family. I was glad she was enjoying what she wanted later in life. She very much deserved time for herself after all the worry and care she'd given me. Now she knew Bruce would be there for me as she had been.

Chapter 11

SURGERY AND DISAPPOINTMENT

JULY 2004

My physical symptoms unfortunately continued, making me feel discouraged. The promise of the ileostomy improving the quality of my life had not happened, which made me even more grateful that Bruce was handling life's responsibilities I'd been struggling with. He took care of Lauren, built the house, dealt with his computer networking business, and was managing our finances. Each challenge he handled calmly while being dedicated to taking care of me. It was almost too good to be true. *Almost.*

One beautiful Sunday afternoon, I insisted on riding bikes because I needed the fresh air and sunshine. We'd ridden bikes together just once, so I thought it would be fun. We had not even ridden a block in our neighborhood before I fell twice. I couldn't keep my balance no matter how hard I tried. He helped me walk my bike back home and put me to bed. I was weak, lightheaded, and extremely discouraged. Why was I getting worse?

I slept for twelve solid hours! It seemed like I needed more and more sleep, but I'd never slept for *that* long. It was 4:00 a.m. when I awoke and Bruce was snoring away next to me, shaking the bed with every breath. He must have left the TV on in our room when he'd fallen asleep. I was shocked to see naked people on the screen. It was obviously a pornographic show. I turned it off and fell back asleep despite the loud snoring. I couldn't keep my eyes open, even after sleeping since 4:00 the previous afternoon.

The next morning when I mentioned what I'd seen on TV, Bruce said that several stations turn to that despicable type of show in the middle of the night and he was going to change our cable service because of it. I was tremendously relieved he was the good Christian man I'd expected him to be, who was so good at taking responsibility for our family.

Three months after we married, after hours of praying about it, I chose to have my entire colon removed. It would be an enormous relief to be done with the ileostomy bag. I hoped getting the paralyzed colon removed would improve my symptoms more than my current situation.

The surgeon explained the many risks involved, but without the surgery my quality of life was looking bleak. I knew I could count on Bruce to take care of me, but it was a burden for all of us. If I could get my energy back, get back to eating normally, I could be more helpful around the house and be there for Lauren when she needed me. Bruce was completely supportive of the surgery.

Depending on Bruce for everything meant he possibly would need access to my bank accounts before I fully recovered from surgery. We rushed to the bank to do the necessary paperwork as we ran countless other errands the day before the surgery. I sighed with relief, knowing everything was left in Bruce's responsible hands.

The procedure was major surgery, and the recuperation was much more difficult than any of us envisioned. I'd been so hopeful that it would finally give me a cure, but sadly, it hadn't. Most days my abdomen was so distended it looked like I'd swallowed a watermelon. It was incredibly discouraging. It seemed like no matter what I did, nothing helped. I wanted to be there for Lauren, who was in high school and needed me, but Bruce was there to fill in the gaps.

I sat both in amazement and with a thankful heart, feeling as though God had blessed Lauren and me with the most amazing man on Earth. He often left me notes of encouragement, scriptures, and words of hope, making me feel cared for and loved. There were so many little extra things he did for me every day, I couldn't recount them all.

Chapter 12

MERGING HOUSEHOLDS

LAUREN'S JUNIOR YEAR (2005/2006)

During Lauren's junior year, I was still suffering with my health issues. I struggled to go to work, but I absolutely loved my department chair position. My employees were great medicine for me to get through the day. Bruce suggested that I take a year off from work, but I didn't want to. It was my dream job! I prayed daily that my physical symptoms would improve, to no avail.

Lauren was busy with cheerleading practices, pep rallies, ballgames, church youth group activities, and hours of weekly homework for her dual credit courses. Bruce was involved as much as he could be and filled in when I couldn't attend, which made me thank God often.

Lauren was blessed with good health, intelligence, and was very pretty. People often noticed her dark, round eyes and easy smile. She would never meet a stranger because she'd befriend them quickly.

Lauren's Jeep

Lauren's biological dad, Scott, surprised her by driving into our driveway on her seventeenth birthday with a brand-new silver Jeep! It was beautiful, and my daughter's smile could not have been any larger if it had been on a billboard. Mom was there to celebrate her birthday and quickly asked for a ride in the new Jeep.

Mom was crying tears of joy when she walked into our house after the ride with Lauren.

She motioned for me to walk into the kitchen and whispered, "I couldn't be happier for you and Lauren than I am today. You both are so deserving of every blessing you receive." She must have turned on the water works because we both stood hugging, laughing, and looking for Kleenex.

Bruce made a huge deal out of Lauren's Jeep, excited to share in the joy of the day. I loved that he was a people person and brought out the best in others. I knew many people who had relationships full of friction and jealousy with their significant others and their ex-spouses. That certainly was not the case with our family. Thanks to Bruce's easy-going personality, he and Scott got along well. Life was not perfect, but Bruce was a blessing.

Later that night Bruce surprised me by asking, "Would it be okay if I ordered a hardtop for the Jeep? It will be more protective than the soft top." I marveled at how thoughtful he'd been to think of my daughter's safety! He went online to order the hardtop right away. How could I be more fortunate?

Bruce had a gentle way about him. He never demanded attention in crowds, was a wonderful listener, and rarely spoke about himself. I enjoyed listening to him as he asked people questions while getting to know them, just as he did when he met a large group of my cousins one afternoon. I admired his humble nature. That was why he chose to have the conversation about the Jeep's hardtop in private. He didn't want the recognition. He was just being thoughtful and protective.

At the time, I'd wished my dad could have known him before he passed. He would have loved spending time with Bruce! I could picture both of them sitting for hours talking and laughing with not a care in the world.

The Portfolio

One afternoon as I was in the living room reading, Bruce called out to me. "Becca, can you stop what you are doing and come here for a minute?" he politely insisted. He turned the computer screen toward me and smiled. He showed me a portfolio that continued to escalate to over two million dollars.

I said quietly, "That is great. Wonderful news."

He beamed at me. "I've never had that happen before." Then he humbly turned off the computer and didn't make a big deal about it. I was so grateful our relationship, or so I thought, was about love, never about money, which is why I thought we didn't often talk about it. Our agreement was to keep the money until we were "old and gray," just as Bruce had said when he showed me the portfolio days before we married.

Around this time, Bruce was combining and cleaning out home and office files, and our bedroom looked like a tornado had come down and blown papers around for hours. I showed him a handful of my old credit cards taped inside a folder for safe keeping. I wasn't in the habit of using them, but it was security for me just in case my medical bills and student loans ever exceeded my budget.

I asked if I should shred them, but he convinced me to keep them, claiming you never know when someone may call and ask you about them. I trusted this advice, not thinking about it again. We continued to co-mingle our papers and files. The naive and trusting part of my soul told me to blend whatever I had with this godly man.

Plastic Tote

During this process I learned that Bruce was a "plastic tote" kind of person, and I was a "filing cabinet" kind of person. I never figured out his system and was perpetually looking for my papers hiding in some tote.

Bruce's response was, "Becca, filing cabinets breed filing cabinets. I would really like to ask you to try to adjust to plastic totes." I decided any organization would be better than what we were dealing with currently.

It didn't make much difference, as our home office continued to be a sea of papers. Bruce's hands were full of responsibility inside and outside of the home, and I certainly did not feel well enough to help. Soon he bought more totes and organized the mess. I held my tongue, wanting to tell him that plastic totes breed plastic totes. However, I decided since he was taking care of our business that his system would work.

Chapter 13

DEDICATED TO THE LORD

Bible in the Foundation

Bruce was what some people would consider to be a sentimental fool. One day he surprised us with a black leather Bible he had purchased and inside the cover placed a wedding picture of the three of us.

"I hope y'all don't mind, but I would really like for the three of us to go to the lot the night before our foundation is poured and together dig a hole for this Bible to be buried."

Later that week, we dug that hole, said a prayer thanking God for our family, our home, and the many ways we would give Him glory as we enjoyed our future home. It was a beautiful evening standing on the fresh soil. Looking at my daughter's youthful smile, I thought my heart would burst with joy.

Bruce's love language was to surprise me with new and unexpected ways he could pamper me. It seemed every time I woke up from a deep sleep, he had added something new to our home's blueprints. The custom designed cabinets, special lighting, upgraded flooring, spray insulation, abundant storage, roomy basement, unique pool house, and elaborate landscaping were all his ideas. He just kept saying, "Our house is dedicated to the Lord."

I remember it like it was yesterday when he and I stood on our back patio watching the landscaper lift huge trees with a crane. Those trees were larger than life, certainly larger than any I had ever had in any of my yards, even after years of growth.

Bruce smiled that cute smile he showed me in high school and whispered, "I just want the best for you, Becca, nothing ordinary."

Bruce almost skipped with excitement as he approached me one ordinary Thursday evening in April. I was almost asleep on the couch when he nudged my shoulder.

He was like a little boy about to explode if he did not tell his secret. "How would you like to go to the Macy's Day Parade this Thanksgiving? I am working with a travel agency and the arrangements are being made as we speak!"

Bruce was over-the-top thoughtful and was always looking ahead, trying to make special memories for our family. He was taking Lauren, Mom, and me on this once-in-a-lifetime special trip. He even asked the agency to book a hotel room that overlooked the parade in case my mom did not want to go outside that morning. Who could be more thoughtful? Mom was thrilled as she told all her friends about her one-of-a-kind son-in-law and trip to the Big Apple. My daughter was beyond excited as she told all her friends about her future trip to NYC. I couldn't thank God enough for the man of my dreams.

Bruce had aged slightly since we were reacquainted almost six years ago, but he was full of energy and ideas, wanting to begin another business on the side that would not require a lot of his personal time.

He explained to me, "I want my key employees to begin installing home theaters since most owners of large homes want them. This business will be in your name, Becca. I think it may provide nicely for us if you decide you don't want to work." Then he insisted Lauren and I create a name for the business. We giggled at the thought of what name we might prefer, but nothing was decided. The love of my life was so considerate.

The school year went by quickly, almost like a New York minute. Before we knew it, the calendar reminded us that somehow it was May. Our house was not quite finished, so Bruce spoke to our landlord who told him we were unable to get an extension on our lease. Bruce said she had rented the house to another family, but he didn't seem too frustrated about it. He rarely got angry about anything. That was one of many things I loved about him.

We were thankful to move into our beautiful house even with numerous items unfinished. Time had passed rapidly, and we were saying goodbye to my precious Lauren's junior year and hello to her senior year, the most important year of all.

Sunday School Roster

Our Sunday school and church friends had been there for me throughout my health struggles, and they celebrated Bruce becoming a part of our church family. I volunteered Bruce to put together a Sunday school roster since he was savvy with computers. Someone suggested contacting our church community when we had a specific repair or need of some kind to promote everyone's business. The roster Bruce was asked to create would have everyone's personal and professional information. We all loved the idea.

Unfortunately, Bruce's work took him out of town often, and the roster took longer than expected to complete. One Saturday afternoon, we got into an argument, which was rare for us. I'd insisted he finish the rosters. People had waited patiently for a long time.

Later that night he walked into our bedroom telling me he had gotten a call from an out-of-town client who was experiencing computer issues. He had to leave to take care of his client.

Before he left, he finished the roster project for the church but had mistakenly left out one column that captured professions as we'd discussed. No one mentioned the mistake to him. They were happy to finally have gotten a roster with names, phone numbers, and photos of each family. I was proud that he had juggled a great deal of responsibilities in different areas of his life and almost never complained. Overlooking the column for professions was a simple oversight and wasn't worth mentioning.

PART 2 – A WORLD I NEVER IMAGINED

Chapter 14

HINTS AT WHAT WAS TO COME

ATM Denial

The morning of May 24 started off like any other day. I was completely unaware of how it would forever change my life when I stopped to pick up some groceries and my ATM card was denied. I brushed it off, like it was just a glitch, and all was well because the store accepted a check, so I wrote one. After I left the store, panic began to set in. I pulled my phone from my pocket and called Bruce as I sat down in the sunbaked car.

His calm, cool, and collected demeanor calmed me immediately. "Honey, it is probably just a mistake. Don't get all worked up. I'll check on it with the bank. Did you pick up what you need for Pam's party?"

"Yes, I did. I'll see you when I get home."

Bruce's reassurance made me feel like he had it under control, and I released the worry, knowing he would sort it out.

I rushed home to decorate the house and get everything together to celebrate Pam's birthday and another year with my precious friend, feeling grateful. Without her, Bruce and I would have never met in high school or become reacquainted later in life. She was a fun cousin for Bruce and a lifelong friend to me.

When the party ended and everyone went home, I finally had a chance to talk to Bruce about the denied ATM card. As promised, he'd looked into it.

"I found out the reason your card was denied. The last auto

draft for your car was the error. The company had drafted $39,000 instead of $390. It was an internal problem, and I will take care of it. I had a similar issue years ago and they sorted it all out." Again, Bruce was an answer to prayer because I knew I did not have to worry about it. I wish I'd been less trusting, but it wasn't my nature.

New Home Purchases

In a whirlwind of unpacking and getting settled in the new house, I made a comment about how much room we had. After about an hour of making a major dent in setting up the kitchen, Bruce suggested we take a break and go shopping for new dining room and kitchen tables.

I was excited, especially realizing how much bigger this house was than anywhere I'd ever lived. It would take some getting used to and some more furniture to make it feel like home. It was a scorching hot day, and we drove over to a nicer furniture store than I normally would have chosen.

When we walked into the store, Bruce took my hand and smiled down at me. "I want you to get anything you desire. We are going to be making a lot of wonderful memories around these tables over the years to come."

I wasn't accustomed to spending such sums, but he assured me it was okay. We found just what we both loved, two beautiful tables where I could picture friends and family enjoying dinners and birthday celebrations together. We picked out a large round table with the most beautiful wood surrounded by ten upholstered chairs. The other table was long and rectangular, with ten large chairs, perfect for everyday use in the kitchen. I envisioned youth groups gathered around both tables enjoying food and fellowship, with Lauren excitedly cozied up with close friends on either side.

Bruce suggested I go sit in the car to cool off while he made the purchase.

"Are you sure?"

He nodded. "You go relax. I've got this." He pulled out his wallet and waved it at me, smiling.

I clutched my purse and made my way to the car, cranking up the AC, happy we were able to afford what we needed for the house and appreciating how much fun it had been spending the day with him.

Builder Issues

One night over dinner, Bruce vented about how our builder had turned out to be a big disappointment. "Have you noticed since we moved in here the construction has nearly ceased?"

I hadn't really thought about it. I'd been preoccupied with unpacking and getting Lauren settled. "I thought you said he was a good Christian man. Are you losing confidence in him?"

He shook his head and set the napkin down on the table. Lauren had already asked to be excused to tackle her mounting homework, so we had a moment to ourselves.

"I'm hoping it's just because he is on a month-long mission trip. I'm rather disappointed that he just dropped the construction responsibilities. Not one subcontractor has been on our property since he left."

I shook my head, sharing his frustration. "I've always heard that building a house was exasperating, but I hadn't expected this."

He stood up and carried his dishes to the sink. I could tell by the set of his shoulders he was irritated, but his voice confirmed it. "It will be okay. I'm sure he'll be back soon and get our work completed." He turned back toward me. "Listen, I don't want you worrying about it. I've got this covered."

I gathered the rest of the dishes and set them in the sink. "Thank you for taking care of everything for us. I admire your ability to control your temper." He was levelheaded even when he had every reason not to be.

He folded me in a hug. "Sure, it's what I do for my family."

Interior Decorator

Bruce's mother had always enjoyed a beautifully decorated home, and Bruce was much the same way. I did my best, but honestly just doing the basics was wearing me out with work and running around with Lauren's activities.

Bruce knew this and asked me later that week, "Honey, what do you think about calling someone in here to help us decorate? We can afford an interior designer. She can help us figure out what to keep and what to toss."

I marveled at the suggestion. I'd never conceived that I could afford such a luxury. "Can we afford this?"

He nodded. "See if any of your coworkers know of someone who can help us."

I asked a few friends for recommendations, and after a week we had a lady knocking at the door eager to help. I felt like a pampered queen.

Family Reunion

Later that summer was my family reunion. I was taking my mother and Lauren for the weekend. Bruce encouraged me to rent a larger vehicle so we could travel in comfort. He couldn't join us with everything he had to do around the house. We were thrilled to have a more spacious vehicle for the long trip, despite it being something far outside of my comfort zone, spending money on such extravagances. I trusted Bruce completely and was becoming more comfortable with a higher standard of living. I wanted Bruce to join us on the trip, but he was determined to use the time to get subcontractors scheduled. He was selfless. He made me so proud.

Chapter 15

BANK NOTE TROUBLE

Mom, Lauren, and I were laughing and singing songs like we didn't have a care in the world, enjoying the ride to see our relatives. We were on the road to the reunion when Dillon James, the loan officer at Bruce's bank, Natural Falls State Bank, called. It was a surprise to hear from him since I'd not been involved in the business matters of the house. I'd only met him once at a football game.

His voice was stern, which was puzzling. "I'm calling because I can't seem to get ahold of your husband. He's not answering any of my calls."

My first thought was Bruce was deep in a project and had misplaced his phone. "How strange."

The one time I'd spoken to Dillon, he was friendly and polite. Now there was an edge to his voice I couldn't quite understand, and it set my nerves on fire. "The note was due at the bank, and the account is overdrawn. Becca, if I were you, I'd pull out the funds from your account to cover things."

Alarm bells rang. Bruce had always taken care of everything. Something was wrong. My heart was beating a million miles an hour and I felt beads of perspiration form on my forehead. Mom was in the car and could hear my end of the conversation. I spoke with an upbeat tone to hopefully mask my concern, not knowing what else to do. The last thing I wanted was for my mother to have a reason to worry about me. I told him, "I'll be home soon and will take care of it right away."

Mom looked at me curiously, so I told her briefly what Dillon had said, leaving out the upsetting way he'd spoken to me as if something terrible was happening. Maybe he'd just had a bad day and was in an unpleasant mood. My intuition told me otherwise, but I had no idea what could have happened to have such an issue with our account.

Missing Money

I had been using Frontier Creek National Bank for ten years, and I'd kept those accounts after we married. I worried about Dillon's tone for the rest of the trip, and when I returned home, I went directly to my bank's ATM. To my utter shock, there was only $525.43 in all my accounts. Where was my money? There should have been at least $45,000 after the sale of my home.

Sprinting into the house, I set my bags down, and Lauren went to the back to start a load of laundry. I confronted Bruce. "What happened to my bank account? I just checked my balance and only have five hundred dollars."

He smiled calmly, as if I was overreacting. "Honey, there must be an error. Remember what happened back in May? A simple mistake. I'm sure everything is okay."

I had no idea what to think. He seemed so sure everything was kosher, but my internal alarm bells were ringing loud and clear. I kept pressing him about the $39,000 missing from my account from the overdraft made in May. Every time I would push an answer, he would repeat that it was simply an internal problem at the bank and Dillon was taking care of it.

He leaned against the kitchen counter, arms crossed over his chest. "You need to just trust Dillon. After all, he has invested too much time into the matter for us to just overstep him and take it into our own hands." Bruce had always spoken highly of Dillon, so I had no reason to doubt what he was telling me. "The man is a good friend of mine, and a mighty fine banker."

I couldn't put the two things together in my mind: Bruce's calm, reassuring words and the stern way Dillon had addressed me trying to get ahold of Bruce. His tone and wording seemed far from someone who had ever been friends with my husband.

Bruce pushed off the counter and walked toward me, arms outstretched. He pulled me close in a hug, and I could feel the reverberation of his chest against my cheek as he laughed. "You are the ultimate queen of worry! Everything is going to be fine, Becca. We are completely fine."

Brain Fog

I had no choice but to trust Bruce. He'd never let me down before, but the nagging worry consumed me. I felt like the other shoe was about to drop. Around this time, I realized my mind was not quite right. At first, I wrote it off as stress just building up with the move and adjustment to a new life with Bruce. But it seemed to be getting a little worse every day. My thinking seemed fuzzier, and I walked down the long hallways at work hugging the walls at times to keep from falling. Coworkers and friends confronted me with their concerns. It was obvious that I was slurring my words and often was unable to remember where I was in the middle of a conversation. My health was getting worse, or certainly my thinking was. Stress alone didn't explain these odd symptoms.

Another Call from the Bank

One afternoon, I was at my desk working quietly. My cell phone rang, startling me out of focus. I glanced at the screen, and a cold, hard fear set my heart beating fast. It was Dillon again. If Bruce was handling it so well, why was Dillon calling me again? My hands shook as I answered the phone.

Dillon didn't grace the call with pleasantries. "Bruce will not answer my calls. Listen, Becca, I strongly encourage you to cash in your investment funds, pay for the house in full, and buy back stocks while they are low."

My mind was racing. I tried to focus on what he was saying. "Please, Dillon, repeat that for me while I write everything down."

I grabbed a pen and captured what he was saying so my fuddled mind would remember and I could relay the message correctly to Bruce. He patiently repeated everything, and I fumed at my foggy mind for not piecing together any coherent questions for Dillon. I had a lot of worries I could have thrown at him, but instead I obediently captured his words and ended the call.

When I got home that night, I confronted Bruce about not answering Dillon's calls.

In his reassuring, calm way he explained, "Honey, I worked all day in the basement of a bank installing a computer networking system. I had no way to get any calls."

I knew there had to be a good explanation why he'd not answered the banker's calls. "I took a note of what he said." I pulled the paper from my purse and read every word. I thought Dillon was talking about Bruce's portfolio, but I would later learn that he was talking about a fictitious money market account in MY NAME at Frontier Creek National Bank, an account I knew nothing about! My stomach was in knots. My gut instinct was telling me something was very, very wrong.

Bruce reassured me, as he always did. "That is excellent advice. I'll take care of it."

I didn't know what to think. My husband, who had never given me a reason to distrust him, seemed to have it all under control. But my gut felt something was not right. I should have listened to my intuition.

Chapter 16

THE MEETING

AUGUST 2006

Weeks later, Dillon called me again, and this time he insisted that Bruce and I meet in his office immediately. Alarm bells were ringing in my head again. Dillon wouldn't be asking us to be there if Bruce had done like he'd said and taken care of this. I left work, panicked and feeling lightheaded. Bruce met me in the bank parking lot ahead of the meeting. The day was pleasant, but I was coated in sweat, anxiety soaking my blouse.

He surprised me by getting in my car. "Honey, I told you a fib about the $39,000 from the overdraft made in May. I was too busy being the general contractor and was low on funds, so I borrowed the money from your account. I was too embarrassed to tell you."

My intuition had been right. Why was he telling me now before the meeting? I was stunned and felt betrayed, but I let him continue.

His voice was strangely robotic, not full of the regret or embarrassment that should have been there. "You have nothing to worry about. I have an automatic draft that will replace it from my own account. I didn't want to cause you any more stress. I've been juggling a lot, but it's all been to take care of you and Lauren."

I was in complete shock. Did he just tell me, as cool as a cucumber, he stole almost $40,000 from me? To top it all off, he lied to me for months about it! He had given no apology. There was no remorse. To him, he was just taking care of business without bothering me. Was I supposed to think, *Oh how considerate of you, dear*? I wasn't sure if it hurt more that he stole from me and lied or that he did not bother to apologize.

I blinked back tears of frustration. "What do you mean you borrowed money from my account? We talked about this and you're only telling me now? Why didn't you—?"

He held up his hand. "They're waiting for us, Becca. We can discuss this later. Let's go." Before I could gather my wits to respond, he opened the door, and as fast as he'd entered the car he left, walking toward the front door of the bank. I shook my head in utter disbelief. I was already anxious, but this conversation had me completely rattled. I opened the car door and stood there looking up at the imposing bank. My body was numb. As I entered the large, prestigious bank, my feet felt like heavy bricks. I was able to walk somehow, but it felt like it was in slow motion.

The receptionist greeted me with a concerned expression and asked if I was okay. "Would you like some water? Are you about to faint?"

I held on to the furniture until I could sit down. Inside Dillon's huge office, eight to ten other people, even more, walked in and joined us at the table. The glass partition allowed anyone in the lobby to see us, but someone quickly came from behind me and pulled the curtains to give us privacy. The tension could have been cut with a knife.

I realized something serious was about to happen, yet Bruce didn't even have a pen and paper ready to take notes, which seemed really odd to me. His attitude was no different than it had been in the car minutes prior to walking into the bank. He was pleasant, detached, and aloof.

One by one, each person dressed in a dark business suit introduced themselves to us. I lost count of how many people were in the room, adding an exclamation point to what a big deal this was. Yet Bruce seemed unaffected.

Dillon cleared his throat and sternly addressed Bruce. "Did you bring a copy of the homeowner's insurance with you?" His expression made it clear he'd expected it to be in his hands.

Bruce made some lame excuse and said he would be happy to bring it to him the next day. Everything that was discussed I was able to hear, yet I felt like I was having an out-of-body experience. My husband had just told me that he had lied to me for an entire month over $39,000. That alone was almost more than my mind could process. My hands were shaking as I held my water bottle.

Bruce remained calm and mannerly with his "yes, sirs" and "no, sirs." While the bankers stayed professional, it was obvious they were extremely frustrated with him. Faces were turning red with anger, and beads of sweat danced on Dillon's forehead.

I remember exactly what I wore that day. It will always be a day that was seared into my mind, even though I have tried desperately to put it all behind me. I had a cross necklace on, black pants, and a silky violet blouse that by the end of the meeting was wet with perspiration. All I was capable of doing was sitting and listening as my world fell apart.

Dillon looked me straight in the eyes and asked, "Becca, what is the appraised value on your home?"

I had no idea. My blank stares made it obvious I had been left out of all the business dealings. He asked me a few other questions that I do not recall, but when I did not have the answers, I shut my eyes and hid my face. I just needed to breathe. The room fell silent. Even with my eyes closed I could feel every eye in the room watching me. My heart was beating so fast and hard I was sure they could hear it. My ears were red-hot, and no matter how much water I drank, my mouth was as dry as a desert.

Trying to keep my voice from quivering, I shared, "I realize that none of you know me or know much about me, but I have recently had my entire colon removed. I have not felt well for some time, but I continued to work. Bruce has taken care of everything for me while I've been recovering." I had everyone's attention, so I continued. "Obviously there are some misunderstandings about our house. Unfortunately, I have no idea what they are." I found my voice and I continued to plead our case. "I am a Christian and I strongly believe in the power of prayer. I would like to ask each of you to pray for us, and for the issues to be resolved."

One of the men in the back spoke softly, "I will pray right now if that is okay?"

I felt like I was watching a movie. A strange one, with an impromptu bank meeting with the curtains drawn and every head bowed in prayer. A lady offered me a Kleenex as the tears rolled down my cheeks.

Dillon spoke to Bruce now, making crystal clear what he expected him to bring back the next day. Then we were dismissed. Every suit in the room sat still as we made our way out of the office. We were the talk of the town, and I had not even realized it.

Desperately I wanted answers from Bruce but just did not have the stamina to comprehend and process all that had just happened. I have no memory of walking out of the bank or getting into my car. Somehow, I returned to work and went through the motions.

When I drove home that evening, I felt for the first time a cloud of disappointment and sadness tugging at my heart. The bank meeting had been perplexing, traumatic, and terrifying, yet Bruce seemed unnaturally unaffected by it.

He blamed the builder for almost everything. "I just did not have the time to keep my business up and running, to be the general contractor that our builder was hired to be, and to fill in all the other gaps, especially since your health issues seem to *just* continue."

His words stabbed my heart. Had he just insinuated my continuing health issues *were to blame*, washing his hands of any responsibility? It made me want to run as far as my legs would allow me to go. I felt betrayed. I hadn't chosen to be sick. I hadn't stolen money and lied about it. Instead of running, I just existed.

Chapter 17

THE KEYS OF DECEPTION

BRUCE'S ILLNESS

Right after the bank incident, Bruce suddenly looked exhausted and was coughing more and more each day. Because of this, he slept in the guest room, not wanting to keep me awake. I was grateful for the space because I wasn't sure who he was anymore. I needed time to process everything Dillon had uncovered.

Thursday, Bruce was ill, but he insisted on working to collect bills from clients. We were building a fence, but there were issues with the man hired by our contractor. Only half of the fence was complete, and even after Bruce made many attempts to talk to the fence contractor, he never returned to finish the job.

I had stayed home from work partially because my concern was growing for Bruce's health. As Bruce was sleeping, I tiptoed into our new office to see what I could learn. Bruce's side of the office was still packed in boxes. We both had a built-in desk, an island in the middle, and shelves to display each of our favorite keepsakes. He'd designed every detail. My side looked relatively organized, but Bruce's was hardly touched.

Alarmed, I found unopened envelopes, old credit card statements with my name on them, and folders Bruce had made for them. I had remembered the conversation we'd had months ago about my old credit cards. He'd insisted we keep them just in case someone called about them.

Missing Keys

My mind was fuzzy. I remember sitting down and just needing

one good, deep breath. Something else had bothered me lately. The keys on my keychain were in a different order, and my post office key was missing. I mentioned this to Bruce later that day when he said that it must have fallen off. I knew better though. The key chain and key were too thick for the key to ever fall off.

My stomach immediately knotted up and I felt my armpits sweat. Something was terribly wrong. Keys don't just fall off or rearrange themselves on a key chain. Before he could protest, I removed the mailbox key from his key chain. "I'll get the mail. You rest up."

Later that day I went to the post office, but there was no mail. I let it go, but now I was looking for suspicious behavior, and I was not disappointed.

The next day or two I noticed he'd taken back his post office key. As I was getting a few things out of the back seat of my car, I saw several keys just lying there on the floorboard, and one of them was a distinctive post office key. Immediately, I drove to the post office and tried it out, but it did not open our box.

Confused and worried, I asked the postman, "May I get an extra key for my box?"

She looked up my post office number and replied, "Ma'am, your name is not on the account, therefore, I cannot give you a key. I am terribly sorry."

No longer willing to play the fool, I confronted Bruce. "What are all the loose keys on the floorboard of my car?"

He looked at me confused. "Are you feeling okay?"

His inference was clear. I was imagining all of this! My gut was once again telling me something was very wrong. Bruce was not to be trusted. I persisted, questioning him about it.

He smiled and reassured me. "There must be some mistake. I'll get you another key tomorrow."

I was feeling sick to my stomach, as if my body was telling me over and over that things were not what they seemed. My mind was muddled; my emotions were all over the place. I went to bed early to escape the confusion. I was grateful Bruce continued to sleep in the guest room.

On Friday, Bruce had gotten worse, so I took him to the emergency room and came home with medicine to treat pneumonia. I put him to bed. Part of me was frustrated and disappointed that he kept things from me. Another part of me felt guilty because he'd always been so caring to me during my illnesses. Didn't he deserve the same? I was terribly confused.

With Bruce out of commission, I began to worry about our house. Still the builder had not finished what we'd hoped. I was frustrated. How was Bruce to work with his computer clients, try to get the builder to get subs to finish our house, and stay healthy? All the pressure had broken Bruce down and gotten him sick. I desperately wanted to see the good in Bruce, the man who loved taking care of us, the man who loved Jesus.

October 2006 Fence Builder

I was sitting lifeless in a chair, feeling numb from head to toe, when the doorbell rang, startling me.

On the patio, an angry man paced back and forth. He was more than a little agitated. "Ma'am, I'm the contractor building your fence. I've not been paid. Can I please speak to your husband?"

A little put off, I explained, "We've just returned from the emergency room. He's sick."

The man seemed unaffected by that excuse, asking again insistently, "May I see your husband, please?"

I left him on the patio outside and closed the door, then walked back to the bedroom. "Our fence contractor needs to be paid."

Bruce confidently told me, "We are going to be funded Monday."

I returned to the man and conveyed Bruce's message.

The man blurted, "Monday is a holiday. How will you be funded on a holiday?"

I shrugged. I didn't know what to think or who to believe. I scrambled, "We will get you the money on Tuesday."

The man's hopes of getting paid went up in smoke. He rolled his eyes and walked away saying words I wish I hadn't heard. Was the pneumonia causing Bruce to be confused? Or was something else going on? My trust in him was failing, and this was crushing me.

I returned to the bedroom and asked Bruce, as he sat up in bed, "I need to know ALL there is about our finances. How will we pay the contractors to finish our home? I know very little, and it is becoming a problem."

Portfolio

He exhaled heavily with disgust. Then opened his laptop and motioned me to look at the screen. I walked to the side of the bed and glanced at the two-million-dollar portfolio that was similar, if not identical, to what he'd quickly shown me months earlier in the rental house. I couldn't be sure because I had just glanced at it back then, fully trusting him. Things were different now.

In desperation, I wrote down EVERY single key he tapped on the laptop and EVERY action he took in a small notebook. I was going to get to the bottom of our financial issues by hook or by crook.

In his usual calm voice, the one that used to be so reassuring but now set my teeth on edge, Bruce explained, "Everything will be fine. All I need to do is liquidate $536,000 from the portfolio to cover the house expenses." He made a big show of all the various ways he had this under control. Later, I hid that notebook from Bruce. Something inside of me knew then he couldn't be trusted.

I was in panic mode. I needed to talk to my mother, my dearest friends, my confidants, but I did not think there was time. Were my fears justified? I had just been surviving with my abdomen healing, but my mind was confused and working overtime. This was all too unbelievable. Surely this was a dream, a nightmare that would end in the morning.

Chapter 18

FROZEN

SATURDAY, BRUCE WAS STILL having difficulty breathing. I was running errands picking up a few things at the pharmacy and going to the bank on a long three-day weekend when everything fell apart. My ATM card was rejected, my credit card was denied, and Lauren's check was not accepted. My hands were shaking as I called my bank, and the representative answered.

"Ma'am, your funds are frozen. Can you call back on Tuesday to get more information?"

"Tuesday? I have to wait three days to find out what is going on with my accounts?"

"I'm sorry, ma'am," was all the woman could say.

I sat in my car with my phone cradled in my lap. I felt like a black cloud was over me and a blanket of darkness was draped over my shoulders. How did life change so quickly? I drove home lifeless, set the keys on the counter, and walked to the back of our closet to kneel in the corner to pray. I cried uncontrollably for most of the night. I was relieved Lauren was out of town enjoying a church retreat and was unaware of how our world was spiraling out of control.

Builder Meeting

The next day I was in the guest room with Bruce when John, our builder, called. I could hear every word, as I was sitting near him on the edge of the guest bed.

He was back in town from his month-long mission trip and spoke with a stern voice. "I need to meet with you and your wife immediately, and it needs to be with both of you." It was a Sunday! I had never known of a builder making calls on a Sunday, but we agreed to meet at a nearby McDonald's. It was odd, since I had not been involved in the building process and I'd not been around him much at all.

On the drive over there, you could have cut the tension with a knife. Neither of us spoke a word. The ten-minute drive seemed to take hours. When we got out of the car, Bruce looked up at the sky and said, "God, thank you for this amazing day." He seemed almost cheerful as we walked into the meeting.

It was obvious during the first few seconds of the conversation John's fuse was lit. He was a short, skinny man with a ruddy complexion and blond, curly hair. His face turned beet red as he asked, "Bruce, can you tell me why you wrote a $49,500 hot check the day I left the country for a mission trip?"

I was in complete shock. I couldn't believe what I was hearing. It finally made sense why no one had worked on our property for over a month! The builder had not been the problem; my husband had.

Bruce coolly responded, "Funds were in another account by mistake. I will work with the bank closely to see that this will never happen again." Was he gaslighting the man?

Once again, my ears heard some of the conversation between Bruce and our builder, but my body was in shock. Sweat rolled down my back. I realized it was not our builder's fault for not finishing our home as previously planned, even though Bruce had blamed him throughout the process. My legs were numb, but when I looked down at my feet, they were walking somehow toward the car, but it was as though everything was in slow motion. I have no recollection of that trip home.

Credit Cards in the Office

That afternoon when Bruce was sleeping, I slipped quietly into our home office and looked at the huge pile of bills stacked on his desk, too many to count. I found one of my unopened credit card statements and tried to log into the account with my usernames and passwords, but I was unsuccessful. I felt an intense, urgent need to flee come over me. Seconds later I found myself in my car driving to my office as quickly as I could. There I could make some phone calls without Bruce overhearing.

I was not able to get information from my own account, which fanned the flames of my unease. As I sat at my desk trying to keep my hand steady to take notes, anxiety built up inside of me and tears rolled down my face. This could not be happening!

The woman checking my credit card initially treated me like I was trying to break into someone else's account, so it took forever to explain what Bruce had done, and why I was trying to figure out what was going on with my account. While on the phone for hours, my world crumbled piece by piece. I'm still not sure how I managed it, but I made detailed notes as I spoke to dozens of people in customer service regarding my account.

Finally, I gave Bruce's phone number to the last lady, and she told me that the contact details were all changed to his information. Then she dropped a bombshell—Bruce maxed out the account. One woman told me that one of the telephone numbers on the account was almost identical to mine other than the last number. This took a sick and brilliant mind to plan. Identity theft is something we may all deal with, but when it is instigated by the love of your life, behind your back, your world abruptly stops. Mine certainly did.

I had trouble driving home because my hands were shaking uncontrollably. No matter how often I wiped my eyes, they quickly filled up again to keep the road ahead of me blurry. Somehow, I got home safely.

Immediately I confronted Bruce with the ugly truth. He was resting in the guest room coughing and coughing. He explained, as he had in the past, that his business was not doing well with all the sacrifices he had made building our house and taking care of Lauren and me after my surgery. He admitted using my credit card but suddenly was too sick to finish the conversation, only after noticing the tone in my voice and face turning red with emotion.

Who had I married? Where was the man I knew? Where was the man who went to church as a boy and who was the pride and joy for his mom and dad as an all-around good guy? What else was he keeping from me? What had happened to the Christian values I thought I married?

I had a million questions to ask Bruce. What were these "things" he'd been taking care of to "help me" feel less stressed?

I started with Lauren's Jeep hardtop he ordered months ago. "Where is it?"

"There was a shipping problem, and it was up north somewhere. I've been calling about it every week."

"What about the Macy's Thanksgiving Day tickets and reservations? Is that going to happen?"

Bruce gave me his travel agent's name. "She's been working on getting your mother's room facing the parade, which has been a challenge."

I stared at him, wondering if anything he told me was the truth.

Chapter 19

THE DAY MY WORLD STOPPED

OCTOBER 2006

My anxiety over the three-day weekend was off the charts. I couldn't sleep or eat. I was a bundle of stress. When I returned to work on Tuesday, I found myself sitting, ironically, in an ethics meeting for all the social workers in the hospital. What I needed to do was skip out and call Frontier Creek National Bank to discuss my frozen accounts, but the meeting was a requirement for my job.

Pay Up

My heart was racing when my cell phone rang and it went to voicemail. As soon as we took a break, I returned the call and heard the immediacy in the banker's voice and began to shake. They claimed I owed $24,000 and if I did not get it to them by the end of the business day it would go to the district attorney's office. I asked if there was a mistake. Surely this was pertaining to someone else's account. I immediately called Bruce, but as usual he did not answer.

As I was driving to the bank, the rain poured down on the windshield. I could hardly see even with my wipers going their fastest speed. I pulled my car over and parked in a dirt lot as I cried uncontrollably. I wanted to call my mother. I wanted her to cradle me in her arms and tell me it would all be okay as she did when I was a child. Only this was no fire that could be so easily put out. I knew comfort would not solve this problem, so I called Bruce's Aunt Karen.

To this day her words echo in my ear. "Do not call Bruce again. Pam and I will meet you at the bank." I couldn't help but wonder what she knew that I didn't. Who was she protecting? Why did she encourage me not to call my husband? My body was just numb. When Pam, Karen, and I walked inside the bank, we were escorted to an office to review my accounts. I was just trying to breathe. This was all too much.

Mrs. Brown, a petite redhead at the bank, showed us three checks made out to my name dated before I married Bruce. "These are credit card checks made out in the amount of $9,900, $25,400, and $13,400." She pressed her lips together and glanced at me. "Your husband deposited those checks into your personal account, then transferred those funds to another account in the Natural Falls State Bank where he got the mortgage loan."

My eyes met Pam's, then in shock I stared at Karen, hardly believing what I'd just heard. Shock showed on their faces. Karen's complexion darkened before she asked a number of questions. I heard none of it. It was like my brain had shut down. All I could think was, *My husband is a criminal. My husband is a criminal.*

Kiting Checks

When Karen finished, Mrs. Brown tapped my arm and explained, "He started writing hot checks from that account. The name for this kind of check fraud is called 'kiting checks,' where checks are misused as unauthorized credit."

I had never heard of that term before, nor did I really understand it even after she explained it numerous times. I was too stunned to think much of anything.

While we sat there making pained expressions, the banker called the money market department and confirmed that three accounts were opened in my name. She gently returned the receiver to the cradle and shook her head slowly. I could tell by her tight-lipped expression what she'd found out escalated things. "I have no idea how this happened. It is impossible to open a money market account online, yet your husband opened them online." She sat back in her chair and stared out the window for a long pause, as if processing what she'd just learned, then turned to me. "Two of the three accounts were opened with zero balance. I've never seen this done before. Accounts are required to open with a minimum of $1,000."

Karen exhaled loudly and blinked away tears. "How?"

Indeed! How was Bruce able to not only fool me all this time, but somehow manage to defraud the bank as well?

Brokerage Account

"I had no idea there were any brokerage accounts in my name." I felt like I'd been punched in the stomach.

Mrs. Brown typed on the keyboard for a minute and turned the screen so we could all see. "You didn't know about this account with $707,417?"

I was shocked; I had never had that kind of money! Bruce had created this false account on the computer and then provided it to Natural Falls State Bank where Dillon worked, in addition to the bank's mortgage company. She later showed me check after check that Bruce forged from not only my account, but also my precious Lauren's account. He had stolen every penny from her account. His handwriting was easily detected.

She cocked her head sideways and frowned. "I'm sorry, Becca. Your money is gone. Your accounts will be frozen. As hard as this is for me to say, you will not be able to bank with us anymore."

Traumatized and numb, I just sat in the chair, trying to breathe. Physically I couldn't walk or talk. For their mistakes, loopholes that allowed Bruce to create false accounts in my name, I was told I would not be able to open another account in that bank whether I had anything to do with the illegal acts or not. I didn't have a leg to stand on because I had added his name to all of my accounts prior to my colon being removed. Karen and Pam escorted me out of the bank's doors shell-shocked. I felt like a criminal, a beaten-to-the-pulp victim, a whipped puppy not knowing where to turn for help.

Pam drove me to her mother's house. Ironically, Bruce did not call me back. He knew when to hide. Karen was furious with June, Bruce's deceased mother. She had been like a sister to her when she married Karen's brother and joined the family decades ago. Karen ranted and raved about how her sister-in-law had known the truth but protected Bruce and could only see the good in him while encouraging our relationship. I had to wonder what was in her heart. Why didn't June let me know? Was it her love for Bruce? Faith I would change the man for the better? It felt like a deep betrayal to me.

That afternoon I gathered strength to do one of the hardest things I have ever done in my life. I had to tell Lauren that we would not be living in the "dream" house anymore and that Bruce was a fraud. We were homeless and penniless in a heartbeat. THIS WAS MY DAUGHTER'S SENIOR YEAR! I had one child, she had one senior year, and it was stolen from both of us. Her dreams of a happy family were trashed, along with our trust in other people.

I gasped for air. The man I had met in high school, grown to trust, loved unconditionally, and vowed to his mother to take care of on her death bed certainly did not know the meaning of the words "love" or "trust." Deception was what he knew well. How had I trusted and married a con artist, and one who was good enough to take advantage of our bankers? He was excellent at it.

Staying at Karen's

We moved in with Karen that afternoon. Lauren and I stayed there for weeks, sleeping in the same bed. My sweet daughter's eyes lost their sparkle. She was in shock as she just went through the motions. I just wanted to hold her all night and rock her like I once did when she was a baby. I told her, "It will be okay," just like my mom told me over and over when I was a little girl watching our house burn to the ground. Yet it was far from okay.

Each corner of Karen's guest bedroom held our belongings, backpacks, clothes, business papers and notes, or schoolwork. We had things stashed in Karen's garage, closets, and in our cars. I felt like we were thrown into the fire and left to turn to ash. Our lives resembled the room, a cluttered mess of everything important to us crammed into one room.

Frozen Funds

The next few days were a blur. Karen paid $24,000 to the bank, trying to keep the scandal from going to the district attorney's office. It never occurred to me to stop my automatic deposit into my checking account at Frontier Creek National Bank. I'm not sure what I thought would happen when my funds were frozen. Yet Bruce didn't let the bank stop him from withdrawing $2,400 from my account the same day it was deposited. Basically, my last paycheck went effortlessly into Bruce's hands.

I nearly screamed into the phone when I spoke to the bank representative. "I was told the funds were frozen, yet my pathetic husband can withdraw whatever he wants?"

She apologized and admitted that this had never been done in their branch. Because we were married, and his name was on the account, there was nothing the bank or I could do to get the funds back. He certainly knew how to play the game and win.

Chapter 20

MY MOTHER'S BROKEN HEART

DREADING TO TELL MOM was an understatement, but I knew I would need to tell her about the horrific news in person before she heard it from someone else. I called my sister, Caitlin, asking her to meet me at Mom's house so she could console her after I left.

Karen and Pam offered to drive me there, and I was grateful, because the state I was in would not make a safe driver for the ninety-minute drive to Guthrie. I was heartbroken, and soon my mother would be too. She had endured a great deal of sadness with my health issues, and I did not wish to add to her burden. I remember her whispering in our kitchen the day Lauren got her Jeep how happy she was for us because of Jackson Bruce Walker. Now I was about to break her heart.

All I could think about was how ecstatic she was when we married. She loved Bruce, as we all did. She had tried to stay strong after my dad died and when my digestive issues erupted. She had given up so much of her life to take care of my daughter and me.

Caitlin and Mom met us at her back door. The minute my eyes met Mom's I started to cry as she held me in her arms. Again, I just wanted her to hold me and to tell me it would all be okay. "Please, Lord, let it all be okay," I prayed.

Karen and Pam did most of the talking. I shredded Kleenex after Kleenex in my hands, as I found it difficult to talk or look at Mom. I felt so sorry for all of us. Karen and Pam adored Bruce; we all did.

My mom sat in her chair hearing the devastating facts. Karen and Pam kept their emotions intact and spoke factually, and I tried to do the same. I knew I needed to be strong and not bring her more worry. She tried to be strong, and we both sat trying to keep our tears at bay. I could sense Mom was feeling more anger than anything else, to overshadow the sadness. Mom hugged me often and reassured me she was there for me, as she always was.

Our visit was short because of the long drive back to Karen's before delving into hours of legal matters. But it was done. She knew what Bruce had taken from all of us. My shoulders were weighed down with guilt. I had deflated her world, just as I had Lauren's. The two people I loved the most I had hurt the most. Our love for Bruce was shattered. The truth stung. The love I thought he felt for us never existed. This haunts me to this day.

Walking out of my mother's back door, I promised myself I would not accept her money to help get me out of the mess. She was a widow and had done enough for me in the past. God would help me find other ways to manage, but it was not going to be through my mother's purse strings.

My sister was there to pick up the pieces and to help our mom. Caitlin shared with me later that sometimes it's easier to feel anger than sadness, especially when you feel helpless. I think that is the world my mom chose to live in at the time. She was furious that Bruce had betrayed me and Lauren, as most of us had been fooled into thinking he was close to being a saint.

Much later in my life my mother conveyed to me that she must have been numb at the time. She couldn't understand why she hadn't insisted on paying for an apartment for Lauren and me. I reminded her if she did insist, I still wouldn't have accepted. She was in shock, and it was all too much to make sense of at the time.

Chapter 21

MY LIFE SHATTERED

LAUREN AND I

During the weeks that followed, the time I cherished the most was when Lauren and I were in bed together. We shut out the rest of the world. I knew she was safe, and I just thanked God for her. When she would sleep, I would caress her hair, hold her close, and pray we would get through this together. It brought me back to when she was a baby lying next to me as I stroked her hair and hummed lullabies. Those were sweet memories. Seventeen years later we were living a nightmare. It was a lifetime horror movie of someone else's life. We did not deserve this; Lauren certainly didn't.

In the fraction of a second, my world had shattered. I had no earthly security, and my life was out of control. I knew the anxiety was building inside of me and a panic attack was hiding around every corner. My emotions were a rollercoaster going up and streaming down, from feeling numb to being outrageously angry. Despite all of this, I had to keep it together to make important decisions.

Lauren was depending on me, yet all I could provide was a shared bed in someone else's house. To help us out, she'd taken a job at a retail store but offered to get a second job, which she did. I was broken. I truly felt strapped financially and raped emotionally. All my daughter's friends were enjoying senior themed functions, finishing high school work, and experiencing a full dose of seniori-tis. Lauren worked constantly and was burdened with a broken heart, with our lives crumbled around her.

I knew I would be okay one day, but I also knew she would never get her senior year back—it was stolen with no remorse. That truth hurt me to the core. I was nearly paralyzed by my guilt, but I knew that wouldn't help Lauren.

If anyone had told me we would be homeless and penniless, I would have told them they were crazy; yet here I was, despite being cautious my entire life, saving money, and working toward my dream job with a solid income. It made no sense.

My mounting problems were like heavy baggage stacked around me, grounding me to the moment. Papers from Frontier Creek National Bank, a notebook full of questions, a journal I had started a few weeks ago, and papers from work that had deadlines to meet were strewn about. Organizing these fractured pieces of my life was something at least I could take control over.

The Purse: A Symbol of My Turmoil

Pam loaned me a large black purse and it became an anchor to my sanity, as strange as that sounds. Oh, how I held that purse close to me! Anxiety was at an all-time high, as I would panic if I couldn't find my keys, so I made sure I put them in a pocket in the purse. There was no telling how many times a day I would look in the pocket to make sure I was not missing my keys. In the midst of chaos, that purse gave me a sense of security. It was never out of my sight.

The minute my eyes shut at night, I saw the ornate key with fringe that Bruce gave me when he proposed. Adrenaline pumped through my veins, and I would have nightmares of thousands of missing keys from the back seat of my car. Then dreams would persist of not being able to find my car keys even after hours of looking everywhere for them.

Detective Sheets

I met with the district attorney's office and the police. Detective Mary Sheets was assigned to my case, and I spent a lot of time with her. She was one of the first people who sat with me, listened to every word that came out of my mouth, and believed me. We spoke daily. Over time I felt like she was family. My insane world was real, and she confirmed it was not a nightmare, that Bruce really had done all of that to me. It was embarrassing, humbling, and alarming, but Detective Sheets helped me survive through the trauma. God assigned her to my case; I have no doubt.

Identity Theft and Forged Checks

When looking at the many forged checks transferring funds to Bruce's bank, his handwriting was unmistakable on the memo lines. He wrote the first one in April 2006.

When I met with the identity theft officer, she instructed me to write to each credit card company to inform them that I had been a victim of identity theft, then file charges with the local police department against the person who stole my identity. I was to give each company Detective Sheets's phone number.

I was to request documentation from the institution asking what they required to become an authorized user of an account in another person's name, to change the mailing address, and to change the contact information. I also needed to find out what information they each had on the account prior to October 2006.

I was to tell them my accounts were changed without my knowledge or approval, which resulted in unauthorized charges. I needed this documentation to pursue criminal charges against Bruce. I was taking notes as quickly as I could with my head spinning.

The identity theft agent explained the bank must suffer a loss before the FBI could get involved. Bruce simply stealing my credit cards was not a federal crime. It was civil. To file federal criminal charges, it often took up to a $30,000 credit card usage. Check kiting was a federal offense, but the feds will only serve a warrant if the bank experiences a loss. It was a lot to absorb.

She recommended I file a fraud affidavit and call Identity Theft 911. It was a free service and would protect my social security number and credit going forward. At this point I didn't know to what degree Bruce had ruined my credit. For now, I needed to make the minimum payment on all the credit card bills.

I was also to monitor Lauren's credit report even though she was only seventeen. We also did a credit check on my mother because Bruce had worked on her computer a few times. Thankfully, he had not gotten to her funds or abused any of her accounts.

Chapter 22

A VILE DISCOVERY

FOG LIFTED

Strangely enough, three days after we moved out of the house, I noticed that my mind was clearer and more focused. My supervisor cried with me as I shared what Bruce had done to us. She told me how much better I seemed, how I was not slurring my words, and I was much sharper than I had been. Other coworkers had commented to her about this as well. It surprised me. Even with all the pressure, my mind finally felt less fuzzy, and for the first time in months I was able to think more clearly.

My world shattered again when coworkers lovingly confronted me with questions like, "Do you think Bruce was slipping something in your coffee? Was he giving you a medication that was not prescribed to keep you from being as alert and aware of what was happening?" Their questions shocked me.

Was it just a coincidence that my clouded mind cleared almost immediately after Lauren and I moved out of the house? I could not help but wonder. Bruce had the opportunity when he gave me my medicine nearly every morning and night. It seemed obvious to everyone around me, including my mother, that I was thinking more clearly than I had in months.

Friends convinced me that I needed to get my hair cut and get it drug tested to confirm their fears. I took their advice and cut my hair, saving the clippings. What I didn't know was how much that test would cost. My attorney told me it would be impossible to prove that Bruce was the person who was poisoning me, even if the test came back positive. I cut my hair for nothing, unfortunately. Despite that, I was thankful the brain fog and sluggishness never returned once I moved out of the house.

Computers

Detective Sheets asked me to collect all our computers and to take them to the police department. I was terrified to confront Bruce, so Pam agreed to come along with me, but I was still afraid. Pam convinced me to call the police and ask for someone to be there while I took the computers. I agreed. My fingers were shaking as I made the call.

The officer who answered told me, "Ma'am, unfortunately because this is a domestic issue, we can't keep your husband out of his own house. If there is no car in the driveway, he's most likely not even there."

Who would have ever thought months ago that I would be calling the police to protect me from the husband I thought was such a godly man? My heart was in my throat as we entered the massive house. It was dark and gloomy, adding to the fear making my heart race. Would Bruce suddenly appear? His behavior had been more than odd lately. I had not been near him since we moved out of the house, yet I didn't know him at all. His behavior scared me. There was nothing he could say or do that would regain my trust in him.

Wiping moisture from my upper lip, I crept down the dark hallway and into our office. I was shocked to find Lauren's computer on Bruce's desk. He had recently said he'd taken it to a repair shop and it would be at least a month before it would be fixed. What was he doing to her computer? It infuriated me that after all we'd been through, he was preying on Lauren through her computer.

We worked quickly to collect everything the police had requested. Sweat was pouring off me from the adrenaline. I glanced at Pam as we pulled away in my car, her fear showing as plainly on her face as I had felt myself. We never looked back as I drove toward her mother's house to drop her off before going to the police station.

I pulled over on the side of the road. I hit the steering wheel over and over with my hands, screaming at the top of my lungs, "Why? Why? Why?" I felt so betrayed and violated by this man I had placed all my trust in. Somehow, I managed to make it to the station, and I left the four computers. A silent prayer was sent up that their investigation would bring us justice.

Two weeks later when they were finished, they called me to retrieve the computers. I was instructed to drive down a ramp and wait for an officer to meet me outside.

The police officer who loaded them in my car looked at me with a sorrowful expression and said, "Lady, I've worked here for over twenty years, and I have never seen anything like what is on these computers. I am so sorry to tell you, but I thought you needed to know the truth."

I could only imagine what they'd found, but I did not have the fortitude in the moment to handle the truth. Later that week, the police officer assigned to my case explained what he'd meant. Bruce was addicted to bestiality. When I was shocked into silence, she continued to explain the definition as humans having sex with animals. She told me that every computer we owned had these types of pictures and videos on them. The thought that the man I loved, shared scripture with, shared a bed with, and brought close to my daughter was addicted to bestiality sickened me.

They also found large amounts of pornography on every computer. I never dreamed there was such filth in our world, much less in our marriage. I kept thinking that this could not be happening; surely this was a mistake.

I thought back to several months ago. Bruce had taken Lauren's computer to make it run faster. She never saw it again. He just kept making excuses about how slow it was and he had to take it in to get repaired. She needed the computer to complete her assignments and write papers, but instead, she had to borrow her friends' computers. This man we both had loved infected my precious daughter's computer with his filth. I was floored.

Gyn Appointment

I immediately made an appointment with my gynecologist to run every test to see if I had contracted a disease from this demented man. Thankfully, God provided me with a wonderful doctor. When I explained why I wanted all the testing done, he cried and prayed with me. After the appointment, I realized I felt filthy.

I drove straight to Karen's house and ran to the guest bathroom to take a bath, then a shower, then another bath as I attempted to scrub away the filth, until my skin burned. I just wanted to feel clean again.

Unfortunately, scrubbing, screaming, crying, and lathering my body with soaps and lotions with strong fragrances could not remove the way I felt. I wanted to run from my own body, but I couldn't.

He raped me emotionally without ever caring or having a second thought. I curled up in a little ball in the shower as the water ran for who knows how long over my back. I sobbed without control until I had no energy to cry anymore. About the time I turned off the water to get out of the tub, I felt dirty all over again. I called out to Jesus, the only thing I knew to do.

It was not until I acknowledged that I had been washed by Christ's blood did I feel clean again. I felt as though Jesus' arms were wrapped around me. I felt His presence and knew I was not alone. As I shut my eyes, it was as though I saw Him beside me, crying with me, hurting with me, loving me as I had never been loved before. I put my trust in Him and in Him alone. I knew that day, that moment in time, that I was clean and renewed. I was a child of the King, and I had no reason to hang my head. He was my Savior.

Chapter 23

LEGAL AND CRIMINAL MATTERS

THE CIVIL ATTORNEY

I was numb with fear about Lauren's future and mine. On October 22, I met with a civil attorney, Mr. Ward, whose office coincidentally was directly across the street from the police station. He was clear while outlining exactly what I needed to do to protect myself. He instructed me to not go back home and to make a report to the following authorities: police, FBI, IRS, and my work's security office. I was to report as the innocent spouse in all activities, then immediately file for divorce, close all my bank accounts, and get small and tight with my budget. We were going to have to survive on very little until this was resolved.

Naive to how things work in the world, I thought the bank would owe me money for not catching obvious forgeries. Mr. Ward explained that because Bruce and I were married, I was liable for any account with my name on it. Every month I was to reconcile my bank statement! All of this sounded so daunting, so complicated. I had not managed our finances before, with Bruce taking over everything in our lives as I recovered from my surgeries. It was one more item on my vast to-do list, adding to my sense of losing control over my life.

The Divorce Attorney

I filed for divorce immediately, not knowing how I was going to pay for the expensive legal bills. I needed a strong attorney and found Harold Phillips. He said two things I will never forget. First,

"The problem is there is no money." The second, "The end of your marriage is now a business problem."

He told me it was going to be an expensive divorce. There would have to be numerous depositions with the builder, fence contractor, both banks, etc. He charged $175 an hour and required a $5,000 retainer to start. I had no idea how I would pay him, but Mom insisted I take a check for $5,000 to help. I appreciated her offer and humbly accepted it. I had no choice. The sooner I could be divorced from him, the better off I would be financially and emotionally. My name was already tainted with his crimes, but as husband and wife he would only continue to find ways to deceive and abuse me.

Days later Mr. Phillips called me. "Becca, you are not going to believe this," were his first words. My heart leapt to my throat. I'd heard this too many times lately. "The constable was unable to find Bruce to serve the divorce papers. He went to the house, rang the doorbell several times after seeing the lights on. A man finally came to the door and said he was Bruce's brother Mike and Bruce wasn't home."

My aggravation ignited again. This was just another one of Bruce's games.

The lawyer continued, "I called the constable and asked for a description of the man who opened the door. As suspected, it was Bruce, not his brother."

Later, I confirmed this by asking Karen to call Mike, who said he'd not been at Bruce's house. This was just another deception to run up my legal bill. The cunning games continued.

FBI Investigates

It came as a complete shock that the FBI was investigating me. This was the first time I'd ever known someone investigated by the FBI, except people I read about in the news. By the end of the ordeal, I had dealt with them so often, I knew the agents by their first names.

Mercifully, the truth was clear to the agents, that I'd been taken advantage of by a criminal. That criminal just happened to be my husband. They knew I was naive and innocent of any wrongdoing.

One of the agents called me after Bruce's initial interview. He wanted to let me know Bruce had brought his Bible to the appointment. During the interview, the agent said he lied so often he asked Bruce to move the Bible as far away as possible because it was clear he only used it as part of his scheme.

That did not shock me. Bruce took his Bible with him everywhere. It was a part of his disguise. It was clear to me Bruce used God to benefit his agenda, which is how he fooled me the whole time I knew him.

Chapter 24

BLESSINGS FLOWED

I CANNOT EXPLAIN THE feeling of living in a beautifully designed and decorated home with my daughter by my side one day, then suddenly having no money and being homeless the next. It happened in an instant.

Jesus' Comfort

One comfort I clung to is I never felt alone. I felt Jesus' arms around me. Even though I could only take one day at a time, sometimes just one breath at a time, I never felt abandoned by Jesus. I thank God for His unfailing love for me then, today, and every day. My relationship with Jesus is like no other.

Reading scripture reminded me of Jesus' words: "I will never leave thee, nor forsake thee" (Hebrews 13:5 KJV).

Lauren's Pain

One night after Lauren was sound asleep, I stood nearby just watching her breathe softly. Her world would never be the same. I was an adult and would get through this somehow, but she was a child. Children were not born into this world to be hurt like this. She had loved Bruce but never even had the opportunity to say goodbye to him, or to yell at him, or to ask why he had done so many hurtful things to us. Desperately, I wanted to take her pain away, yet I couldn't. I felt guilty. People could hurt me, but when they hurt my daughter, that was a different story!

Humbled, Homeless, and Broke

Broken and humbled, I was awake most nights. I'd worked so hard my whole life. Sacrifices I thought would be difficult were nothing now. I quit my Sonic Diet Coke habit in a split second because spending money for anything like that was out of the question. I remember later getting Sonic gift cards from friends and coworkers. You would have thought I was a child given candy once again. I would make the Diet Coke last as LONG as I could.

The little things in life I once took for granted were too luxurious for my wallet or new lifestyle, but I tried to remind myself that I would always have Jesus and He paid the price long ago on the cross, not me.

Sister Tribe

I called Marilyn, one of my closest friends, to update her on what I was going through. An hour later she texted me that my "Sister Tribe" wanted to meet me after work. Marilyn was referring to a close group of our friends, mainly divorced single moms. We were not merely friends of acquaintances, but a family who could count on each other no matter what.

I sat with my Sister Tribe in the outdoor courtyard of a fast-food restaurant accepting their hugs and reassurances. They were not going to allow me to go through this nightmare alone. Each friend slipped an envelope full of cash in my hand. These single moms, I am sure, needed the money for their own families, but they did not hesitate to share what they could. They made it clear if I needed more, they would be there for me.

These dear friends gave me more than money. They provided me with the gift of loyalty throughout the turmoil that followed. I was blessed and reminded that the scriptures state, "Let us not love with words or speech but with actions and in truth" (1 John 3:18 NIV). These ladies remain my sisters at heart and have loved me and inspired me through the darkest of days. I thank God for their genuine friendships.

Aunt Lou

I was in a desperate way. I knew Bruce had taken all my money, racked up bills I couldn't cover. I was already living off the generosity of others. How was I going to afford to divorce Bruce to clear my name? Legal fees were adding up quickly. How was I to put gas in my car, pay for phone bills, food, and other necessities?

My hands shook as I called Aunt Lou, one of my closest relatives, and shared my situation with her. Embarrassed, humiliated, scared, and desperate, I knew she would know how to help. Aunt Lou always made me feel like the most important person on Earth. She hosted all the family's crazy Christmases, greeting each family at the door dressed as a clown, Mrs. Santa, or some other fun character. I was invited every summer to spend a week with her daughter, my closest cousin, Ann.

Crying uncontrollably the minute I heard her voice, I tried to talk to her but was too choked up to get the words out when she interrupted me. "Becca, I'm not sure what you are going through, but it sounds worse than I can imagine. Please know that I love you and my money is the Lord's money. I'm happy to share it. I will be in touch with you tomorrow after I talk to my banker. If you need more, call me. Remember, I love you. Everything will be okay." She didn't cry or pity me. Instead, she gave me hope.

You never forget people like that. The people who show up in the worst of times with the sweetest words and supportive actions are the genuine hands and feet of Jesus. How precious her words were to me.

Gifts from Chad's Family

One bustling Friday afternoon, as exhaustion crept upon me after a long day's work, my phone jolted me from the brink of sleep. It was Sally, my mother's cherished friend who had relocated to our community a few years when she married Chad Bower, someone I considered my adopted uncle.

"I need you to come over to the house. Please?" Sally insisted.

I couldn't help but be curious. Her tone was unusually cheerful but curt.

I found myself driving to Sally's, not remembering which route

I took or if there were green lights I sped through. My mind floated back to my childhood. Chad's infectious laughter always brought a smile to my face. Back in the day, Chad, his late wife Brenda, and their children Rick, Kaci, and Sharla were fixtures in our weekend plans. Whether hosting us at their home or visiting ours, our families were inseparable during my childhood. My mother and Brenda shared an unbreakable bond, often found side-by-side sewing, cooking for church events, or organizing memorable evenings for us all. The news of Brenda's passing from cancer came as a profound shock, given the enduring presence she held in my life since chi ldhood.

When Chad met Sally several years later, he was quick to marry her. It was obvious their laughter and love for one another brought joy to us all. Sadly, Chad only lived a few years before dying unexpectedly from a heart attack. Chad's kids were grown and now, without their mom or their dad, were very close emotionally to Sally.

Suddenly I realized, my car was parked on Sally's driveway. When I arrived, she took me by the hand and walked me into her kitchen with a smile on her face and happy tears in her eyes. There were four checks on her counter, all made out to me from Sally, Rick, Kaci, and Sharla. How I wished I could hug them all for their generous gift. The memories I had made with these three while growing up were priceless. I cried a river in Sally's kitchen and couldn't quit. I hugged her tightly and did not want to ever let go. She cried with me and assured me I was not alone.

That night I fell asleep holding my purse and the four checks inside it as if my life depended on it. The generous funds they lovingly gave me helped pay for legal fees, at least for a while. I thanked God that friends can truly be Jesus in the flesh, as I felt their love like I never imagined.

Chapter 25

GOING THROUGH THE MOTIONS

GATHERING THINGS FROM THE House

We had left so much behind at my "dream" house. I made a trip to retrieve some of our things. Pam and Karen agreed to go with me. I texted Bruce and told him what we were doing and made it clear I did not want him at the house. He agreed to be out of the house when I arrived, but I no longer trusted anything he said.

Karen drove, and my heart raced as I sat in the car on the way over to the house. I wiped my sweaty palms on my pants, dreading being back in the house where he now lived. We entered the house together on guard, expecting Bruce to appear around every corner. I zipped through the house, grabbing clothing, toiletries, and papers from the office, and ran to Karen's car quickly, not even knowing if I locked the front door.

As we drove away, Bruce's gray SUV came out of nowhere and pulled up to us. He rolled his window down and stared at us with the glassiest eyes I'd ever seen. He didn't say a word, but just stared.

We sped away, not sure what he was capable of doing. Karen turned to me, her eyes wide with shock. "He must be on drugs. Did you see his eyes?"

It looked that way, but Bruce on drugs? It was hard for me to fathom the man who had shown me such godliness, who had prayed with me, was on drugs along with all his other vile behavior. Yet I had never seen him look like that. Bruce was a stranger, a person who had only pretended to love me as long as he could benefit from our relationship. Surely a demon was behind those eyes.

Bruce Reaches Out

One of the first days Lauren and I were staying with Karen, Bruce came to her house to talk to me. It was the only time I remember Bruce in a panic. I hid in the kitchen as she answered the door and told him I was not there. My heart was racing as they talked about his urgent need to discuss something about insurance with me. I was relieved when I heard the sound of the door shutting after a quick goodbye. I had not been prepared for him to randomly show up and demand to have a conversation.

Karen was cool as a cucumber. I know she wanted to scream at him, but she also wanted him to leave as quickly as possible. I couldn't help but remember that her son Bobby had died in a car wreck years ago, when Bruce became almost a second son to her. Karen had lost her parents, her husband, her son, June, her brother Robby, and now she had lost Bruce, but in a completely different sense. My heart ached for her.

Letter from Bruce

The next week, I received a letter from Bruce. My hands shook as I read every word, rage boiling with each paragraph.

Becca,

I'm writing to you because I cannot reach you by phone. I have sinned against you and our marriage. I have sinned against God and myself. I lied to you about our debt, and with these lies, I have hurt Lauren by putting you both in danger. Now you are at serious risk from debt, the court, and a painful humiliation that caught you unaware. I know you must feel out of control to resolve these issues.

I am so sorry for hurting you. I know my actions have scared you and you are already so vulnerable. You are so full of grace and innocence. I was not.

Every hour of every day I am struggling with the pain and anger that you must be feeling. I hear and think about your angry words every hour of every day. There is no way I can force them aside to live my own life. Now that I am cut off from your words and thoughts, it is even worse. I should have known that someone who inspired such a great love, one greater than I've ever known, would have such a great effect on me.

I will not stop until I have corrected the financial and other wrongs I have done. I know it won't change these wrongs, but I do not want you to worry about being left to deal with the disaster I've created for you.

I'm struggling to understand every day why I did this to you, why I made these choices that have caused you so much pain. A lot of these troubles stem from my insecurities about my physical self and haven't felt I was worthy of you. That was from my insecurities, not from your actions.

I grew up in a family that was good with money, my father especially. I've never quite gotten a handle on money, and wished I was more like my dad. He was conservative but didn't mind risking a lot for a large gain, partially spurred on by a competition with his siblings they never spoke about.

Because of this, my brothers and I have adapted to living with a higher level of risk for that big reward. I am guilty of not allowing you to learn of my risks and participate, making decisions you were comfortable with. Despite what you've seen, I am able to handle our finances and make a good living. You've seen it at times. I should have shown you more respect than I did. I am sorry I didn't match the respect you showed me .

You've asked me a lot of questions about how I differ from my brothers Mike and Doug. I have some definitive answers for you. You've asked me about my previous marriages, but there is no comparison to what we've had. I am willing to go as deeply as you or anyone wants on that topic. I'm still processing and understanding more as every day passes.

I hope and pray you can feel this in my voice and see it in my eyes. I want you to remember this isn't all of me, all of you, or what we have built together. I miss you terribly, more than you will ever know.

I am sorry.

I love you, Bruce

Given everything I knew about Bruce and his fraud against us, the vile things we found on our computers, especially my daughter's, his words all rang hollow. I was more determined than ever to untangle our lives from this despicable man.

Chapter 26

BRUCE LURKING BEHIND THE SCENES

STALKING

Bruce would appear seemingly out of nowhere, but we never found a tracer on my phone or car. Each time I looked up, surprised to find him there, my heart dropped. It took every ounce of self-control not to lunge at him. I knew that was the game he was playing.

My body may have looked normal on the outside as I went to the grocery store, church, and work, but I always was looking over my shoulder, afraid to see Bruce at every turn. It was exhausting mentally, physically, and emotionally.

Lauren's SAT

Lauren was scheduled to take the SAT exam one Saturday during this chaotic storm. Her close friend's family, the Steiners, invited us to spend the night before the test. My hope was that Lauren could go to bed early and get the rest she needed to focus on her exam. It was also nice to be away from Karen's house, to be with friends who laughed and got our minds off the mess we were dealing with.

I did a double take when we saw Bruce in his car down the street from their house! How could Lauren get a good night's rest with this man stalking us and infringing on our privacy? I was boiling with anger!

I called Detective Sheets, who sent a patrol car to sweep the area. Bruce was nowhere to be found by the time they drove by the house. Nobody slept much that night. I was furious that Lauren's life was now reduced to this, by the man who once posed as her father figure, and one who claimed to be a person full of faith, burying a Bible under our home's foundation.

I'll never forget the day Stefanie Steiner, Brenda, her mother, Lauren, and I went to Kaci's Fashions, a local department store, to get the girls each a dress for a school function. As we shopped, I realized Bruce was staring at me. I looked straight in his eyes, then looked away as if he'd been caught. We immediately left the store as he walked to one of the checkout lines.

After telling my attorney all the places that he showed up when I was around, he advised me to get a track phone. I decided to lock my cell phone in the filing cabinet where I worked and bought a burner phone with limited minutes. I copied all my contact numbers into a notebook, taking an outlandish amount of time. The notebook of contacts was one of many things I kept in the black purse Pam had loaned me. I carried it everywhere I went, as if it were a life vest.

The Phone Call

One morning I answered the phone at work and was surprised to hear Bruce's voice on the line. He knew that was the only place he could reach me because I wouldn't talk to him otherwise.

"Becca, we need to talk."

Fear gripped my gut, and I debated about hanging up the phone, but instead I tried to keep my temper in check. "I need your attorney to call mine."

"I don't have a lawyer, Becca, please. Can we just talk? What should we do with the house?"

This was the first time I'd heard his voice in a while, and it put me in a state of panic. "You need to call Dillon at the bank and deed the house to me. You need to give me everything. And please..." I tried a deep, calming breath. "Stay away from Lauren. You are despicable. Absolutely despicable!" His deep breathing and evil attempt to be sincere would never be enough to right the wrongs with what he'd done to us.

Bruce kept a calm tone, almost consolatory, but it only made me angrier. "I feel horrible about how I have hurt Lauren. I don't know what you have told her, but please let her know—"

I interrupted whatever he was going to say. I did not want my daughter's name in his mouth. "YOU ARE DESPICABLE!" Then I hung up on him. I called my divorce attorney immediately. He said the call was not quite a threat, but he would consider it harassment.

Chapter 27

SECRETS GALORE

FAKE PORTFOLIO TO BANKER

Several days later, I met with Dillon and another man assigned to our case. I pulled out a copy of the fake two-million-dollar retirement portfolio and showed it to Dillon. The shock was visible on his face as he took off his glasses, rubbed his eyes, and then looked at the paper again. My quick thinking had allowed me to reveal the fake portfolio scheme to Dillon. It contained no stocks or bonds, only a fictitious document Bruce created to lure me into his sick game. It is hard to wrap my head around his deception. Did he consider I might find out about such a large, fabricated portfolio? What was his plan if I ever found out about the three bogus money market accounts he created in my name with over $700,000 in one of them? Who does such a thing? Only a deranged con artist would.

Secret Fiancée

Bruce devastated me with his lies about our financial situation. As difficult as that was to come to terms with, the breadth of his deception would slowly unravel before our eyes. Every week a new, more horrific revelation was uncovered.

The next day after work, I drove to Karen's house, our temporary home away from home. She was white as a sheet when I walked in the door. Once I got settled, she took a deep breath and said, "Becca, I need to share something with you that I learned today. You will want to sit down to hear it."

I panicked. Hadn't there been enough surprises through this

whole process? I braced myself for more upsetting news.

Karen explained to me that she had just called Mike and Kay, Bruce's brother and his wife, to share the disappointing news about Bruce. Kay then shared what had transpired before our wedding and what caused her "migraine." She shook her head and looked at me with sympathy. "Bruce's first wife, Anne, called Kay two days before your wedding saying she'd been trying to contact Bruce but he wasn't answering his phone. She was worried about him."

I sat back against the couch, bracing myself. I could tell this was something upsetting by the haunted look in Karen's eyes.

She continued, "Kay told Anne that Bruce was doing great, in fact he was getting married in two days. Anne didn't respond for a few seconds. Apparently, she was shocked at that news." Karen cleared her throat.

Just get on with it, I thought. The anxiety of what was coming was destroying my already delicate stomach. Given Bruce's latest shocking behavior, it literally could be anything.

Karen shook her head, "Anne's voice was shaky, and finally she asked how Bruce could be getting married. She told Kay she'd gotten back together with Bruce over a year ago and they were planning to get remarried."

My ears heard what Karen had said, but nothing sank in. I stared at her blankly, not wanting to process it.

Karen pressed her lips together and she blinked away the gathered emotions. "Kay was floored. Later, Anne forwarded emails that proved every word was true, they had an intimate relationship for over a year. It turns out, Becca, he was engaged to both of you at the same time." Karen reached out and touched my arm.

Tears formed in my eyes, and I reached for a Kleenex.

"They had been dating the entire time you were with him!"

My mind exploded with rage. All those *business trips* were really getaways to visit Anne, who lived just a few hours away. Anne had not known about me, and I surely did not know about their renewed relationship.

Karen took my hand and squeezed it. "I'm sorry to be the bearer of more bad news. I about fell off my chair when she told me."

Tingling from head to toe, I didn't know how to react. It felt like a Lifetime mystery movie. The plot just kept getting thicker and more unbelievable. Except it was *my* husband who led a double life from the time we were reacquainted. Our friendship and marriage, what I thought were based on a love we shared for Jesus, were insidious lies.

"There's more." Karen forced herself to continue, sitting up next to me. "Anne said he'd told her two days earlier he had a major leg injury while installing a computer network system. He claimed glass broke and sliced his leg open and he went to the emergency room, but he was home now. He insisted Anne stay home and not come to help, even though she wanted to be by his side. Bruce told Anne he preferred to be alone and all he wanted to do was sleep."

I stared in disbelief. While he was supposedly in the hospital, we were preparing for our wedding and honeymoon.

She continued, "After two days of not being able to reach him, Anne called Kay to find out how he was doing. Apparently, he was doing well because he was two days away from getting married."

Once again, the world stopped. Fury mixed with confusion. Why didn't Kay warn me before the wedding? It was no wonder Kay had a "migraine" as she watched me and Bruce say our vows. Only a sociopath would try to convince his ex-wife—now fiance—he was badly injured while marrying someone else.

Karen revealed the answer. The day before our wedding, Bruce had convinced his two brothers that I was well aware of Anne and their relationship, but I chose to marry him anyway. Seriously? Who in their right mind would overlook their fiancé's affair and agree to marry anyway? What mother would subject their child to someone who had been living a double life?

As Karen explained it, Bruce's brothers had decided they would stay out of our business and not say anything to me about Anne. Who chooses to sit in a pew and say nothing to protect an innocent child, my daughter, just to keep the peace?

This also explained why his other brother, Doug, and his family chose not to come to our wedding. Again, another missed opportunity for someone to warn me what was really going on. Since then, I've often wondered why one of Bruce's brothers or Kay didn't pick up the phone to congratulate me and lead the conversation to share the truth they knew, the truth Bruce convinced them that I knew. How different my life would have turned out if they'd just taken the time to check in with me before he ruined our lives. We would have been hurt, yes, but he *wouldn't* have been able to do so much damage.

I still wonder why he chose to marry me and not Anne. My friends suspected he was trying to poison me, and it would be difficult if not impossible to prove. They also questioned if he may have had a life insurance policy on me that I knew nothing about. My mind was racing with their suspicions. I just wanted the nightmare to end.

I'd never had harsh words for Pam or Karen. They'd helped me and Lauren so many times over the years. Soon Pam joined us, summoned by her mother, and the fury continued. Her eyes were swollen from crying and her face was red and splotchy.

Pam sat next to me on the couch and took my hands in hers, her look almost destroying me. "I'm so sorry, Becca."

I squeezed back. "I'm sorry, too." A swirl of emotions coursed through me. Pam had been my best friend since childhood. I wanted her heart to heal too.

Karen remained pacing the floor. "What I don't understand is why June encouraged y'all's relationship?" It was difficult watching Karen get so mad at Bruce, knowing her heart was as broken as mine. I understood how she felt if anyone did.

Pam just shook her head and looked down at our clasped hands.

Karen repeated herself several times, "Why would June do that?" I'd been wondering the same thing. Why hadn't she protected me from her son?

Then Pam joined in, fanning the flames. "She had to know Bruce was taking advantage of her funds and had many other problems." She had adored Bruce, who quickly became a second brother to her after Bobby's death almost ten years ago. The tragic car accident changed Pam's life forever, yet Bruce helped put a smile on her face. Now that smile was gone. Only a look of deep sadness remained. My heart broke for her, too.

Karen stopped pacing and pointed at me. "She loved you, Becca. I just don't understand why she didn't protect you from Bruce."

The three of us sat soaking in the disappointment and fury, realizing the Bruce we'd all grown to love was not the man we'd thought he was. Moments later, Karen held her head, then raised her hands to the ceiling. "It is hard for me to believe this. I thought Bruce was more responsible after I bailed him out of jail the second time!" Karen had lost herself in anger, and it was as if she'd forgotten I was sitting right there in the room.

Utterly shocked, I found my voice and asked, "Karen, did I hear you correctly? You bailed Bruce out of jail...twice?"

Wiping the tears from her face, she turned to me. "I am so sorry I never told you. You both looked so happy, and I truly thought Bruce was learning how to be more financially responsible."

Pam was fuming and struggled with what she'd just learned about one of her closest cousins. "I just can't believe Bruce would do this. Mom, why didn't you ever tell me about that?"

Her answer never registered in my mind. All I could think about was my daughter could have been spared all of this if they'd just told me the truth. I would never have married Bruce had I known he'd been in jail. Pam destroyed me further with what she said next.

"Didn't Bruce learn his lesson when he was married to Anne and had the affair with Janene? He saw what that did to her."

The bombs kept dropping. I tripped on this new layer of betrayal, wondering if I'd heard her correctly. "Why didn't either of you ever tell me about Bruce going to jail? Did you just say he cheated on Anne? You never thought to tell me this before I married him?"

They exchanged glances, then looked at me for a few heartbeats. Karen finally said, "I just assumed you knew."

At that point, my body was numb from everything the day had thrown at me. Her words echoed in my ears as I ran to Karen's guest room, where we'd been staying, and fell on the bed. Neither of them had mentioned anything close to this the entire time I was with Bruce. It never occurred to them to mention the hot checks, jail time, or Bruce's cheating. It only came out when everything in my life was crumbling around me. I felt so betrayed. Why would they protect him and leave me out to dry?

My mind raced with so many questions. Why had Pam asked me not to break Bruce's heart when she first learned we were spending time together? What other skeletons were in Bruce's closet that I, his wife, had no clue about? How in the world did so many people sugarcoat his misdeeds as if they didn't matter? They kept all of this from me until it was too late. That question continued to ring in my ears. There was no one I could trust!

The Time at Karen's

The last few weeks while living at Karen's house, I knew we were all just existing. Karen and Pam loved Bruce and were devastated to realize how serious his recent mistakes were. They'd been so happy when we married. Now they were heartbroken and angry, just as Lauren and I were.

The irony was bittersweet. Bruce's family took us in when I needed help. As disappointed as I was with Karen and Pam for keeping things from me, Karen *had* taken care of me the day my house burned when I was six, and now she was giving me and my daughter a place to stay decades later. It was obvious that Jesus was looking out for us.

Berks' Offer

Karen, Pam, Mike, and Kay had all been scammed by Bruce as well. No unkind words were ever said between us. However, by this time, it was becoming uncomfortable staying at Karen's house with all the baggage between us. We all needed a break from one another, at least for a while. What a sweet surprise it was when my phone rang and I saw Anna Berk's name pop up on the screen. "Becca, Steve and I want you and Lauren to come spend the weekend with us. You are welcome to stay longer if you choose. We just want to be here for you in any way, whatever makes your life e asier."

Of course we jumped at the chance. That first evening, Steve was outside watering the lawn when he saw Bruce's car at the end of the block. He was gasping for air when he walked into the house, trying to find me. I felt sick to my stomach.

"Becca, Bruce is right down the block sitting in his car! What a creep!"

I opened the curtain to glance outside and saw his familiar car hiding in the shadows.

What was his game this time? I was so looking forward to relaxing at Anna and Steve's, never imagining Bruce was lurking nearby. My phone was locked in my cabinet at work. How was he showing up wherever we were? What was his sick game? I worried about his intentions and felt guilty about bringing my friends into the fray.

Chapter 28

GAMES

PLAN TO EVICT

In November, I was working closely with Dillon and other bank representatives, knowing that they wanted Bruce out of the dream house as soon as possible. He'd never provided the bank with a homeowner's insurance policy, putting the bank at risk. I was nervous when I picked up the phone and silently rehearsed what I was going to say to Bruce. Before I thought too hard about it, I dialed his number and held my breath. When he answered I didn't bother with courtesies.

"You need to get out of the house immediately. My job as Lauren's mom is to protect her. What she needs is a sense of normalcy. Since you did this to us, you should be suffering the consequences of your actions, not the other way around." I knew my daughter and I would never live there again, but I needed Bruce out of the house. "It is the least you can do."

When he hemmed and hawed, I bit my tongue, just wanting him out of there. I didn't want to anger him more than necessary, because when it came down to it, he had to leave of his own volition. I just wanted to be done with all of this, but there was no way out but forward, through the mess he'd created.

"I'll be out in a week, Becca. You have my word."

I notified the builder, John, who was prepared to put new locks on the doors immediately.

Meanwhile, Dillon encouraged me to continue pursuing a divorce and insisted Bruce deed the house to me. I might be able to sell the house and get the money to pay off the bank, but it would require an extension of the loan. He explained if I could get $75,000, I could pay off the note, get the deed in my name, and sell the house. He could have said one million dollars just as easily; both figures were equally impossible.

Detective Sheets confirmed Bruce's computer business was not in good standing with the IRS as of January 2004. I hoped this would help me keep the house if I could get things sorted with the bank. I talked extensively to Detective Sheets about all the forgeries Bruce wrote in our accounts at Frontier Creek National Bank. She explained that my bank still didn't know how Bruce created the three false accounts.

It was obvious that he used his intelligent mind to swindle others rather than work. Playing hurtful games with innocent people was what he chose to do with his time.

PART 3 – MOUNTING LEGAL TROUBLES

Chapter 29

ARREST WARRANTS

ARREST WARRANT

Rushing to finish a pile of work on my desk, I almost ignored my cell phone ringing. When I saw who was calling, I shook my head. What now? "Hello, Detective Sheets! How may I help you?"

"Becca, I'm sorry to tell you some disturbing news. I wanted you hear it from me, rather than find out another way."

Alarm bells rang in my mind. "What is it?"

She took a deep breath and dove right in. "There is a warrant out for your arrest."

I almost set the phone down, thinking it was a prank call, but I knew her voice. "Excuse me. Who has a warrant out for their arrest?" She must have misspoken. It should be Bruce in jail, not me.

"Yes, YOU do, Becca. There is no easy way to tell you this. It stems from an outstanding traffic ticket you apparently never paid."

Trying to not scream or panic, I just sat numb, fumbling with the idea of going to jail. "What traffic ticket? Detective Sheets, please tell me I'm not going to jail! My daughter needs me." Everything felt like it was spinning out of control. I forced a few deep breaths as the detective explained what needed to happen.

"Becca, I think you need to get legal representation so you can sort this out."

We talked for a few minutes, but I have no recollection of them. All I knew was this had to be fixed. I would be on the hook for more legal expenses when I already had no money.

I hung up the phone and laid my head on the desk to stop the room from spinning. I wanted off this merry-go-round of chaos. I shouldn't be the one going to jail. My daughter would be left to fend for herself while Bruce played games with our lives. Anger flared and nausea erupted, churning my already sensitive stomach into a stress-fueled mess.

Right away, I met with my civil attorney, Mr. Ward, to get more information about the warrant. As we talked, I realized what must have happened. Back before the initial call with the bank when everything blew up, I'd borrowed Bruce's car to run errands. I was shocked when I was pulled over; the red lights and siren in my rearview window scared me badly. I'd rolled through a stop sign. When the policeman wrote out the ticket, he asked me for my license, insurance, and proof of registration. I could not find anything in the glove box. The officer added fines for missing proof of insurance and an expired inspection sticker. I couldn't afford to take off work anymore to pay the ticket, having used up a lot of my personal time with my illness.

When I got home, I walked into the house frustrated with Bruce. Failing to stop was my fault, but how irresponsible was he for not taking care of the inspection sticker and insurance? He was showing me an ugly side to his character I hadn't seen before, raising red flags in our marriage. This was my first glimpse into his true nature. Little did I know at the time it was just the tip of the iceberg

"Bruce," I called out when I returned home. When he called from the office, I joined him and told him what happened. "How did you let the insurance and tags expire?"

Bruce was calm and reassuring. "I've just been so busy. Listen, don't worry about the ticket. I'll take care of that since it was my fault for not keeping up with things." His calm demeanor and reassuring words allowed me to relax a bit. "My attorney friend owes me a favor. He'll help me square it away."

When I asked him why he'd let both lapse, he gave me random excuses, but my mind was fuzzy back then and I just couldn't process everything, so I never pushed the issue. He was taking care of it, that was what was important. Later in the week he reassured me it had been taken care of when he showed the insurance policy to his attorney friend. He'd flat out lied. He ignored the ticket.

I explained the entire scenario to my attorney, and he confirmed I really did have a warrant out for my arrest! Bruce let his insurance and registration lapse, but because I was driving the car, it was my responsibility to pay the fine.

None of that mattered now. Mr. Ward told me even if I'd paid for my ticket, I still had no insurance on the car involved. My driver's license would be suspended. Looking back, I also understand why Bruce wanted me to rent a car to go to the family reunion. It allowed him to drive my car while I was out of town and avoid getting caught like I did. I braced myself for more fallout from Bruce's heartlessness.

Backdate Auto Insurance

Weeks later, I was purposefully introduced to Bruce's insurance agent, who was eager to meet me to share Bruce's true character. "It is difficult to share the truth with you, but you must know that Bruce came to my office soon after you were separated. Bruce was frantic, saying that you would leave him if I did not backdate his auto insurance. As you can imagine, I told him what he was asking me to do was against the law and therefore I was unable to comply with his request."

I stared at him, not sure how to respond.

He saved me by continuing. "I told him that what he was asking me to do was against the law and I just couldn't help him. I'm sorry, but I felt you needed to know." His words weren't laced with anger, but he probably had been bothered that Bruce put him in that position. That explained the day he came to Karen's house in a panic trying to talk to me but Karen told him I wasn't there.

How did the man I once married think nothing about disrespecting the law? Where were the morals I thought he had? More acting. More games.

As we were digging for truth, we discovered there was also a warrant for Lauren's arrest. Several months earlier, she'd also been pulled over and received a traffic ticket. Bruce said he'd taken care of it that same week, through his attorney friend, when truly nothing at all had been done.

I was livid! Did he think I would never find out? My seventeen-year-old daughter had a warrant for her arrest because of his lies! His treacherous behavior was despicable. Only a sociopath would do this to people they "love." Were there any words that came out of his mouth that were not lies?

He'd harmed me, but when I learned his lies were affecting my daughter's life, I felt rage for the first time in a long time. Both my body and mind had been numb for months. I couldn't remember the last time I felt any emotion. But now I felt rage...REAL RAGE.

Forging his name on my accounts, putting my name on false collateral, and stealing money from my bank accounts were bad enough. He'd also forged his name and taken all of Lauren's money from her account as well. He had lied and did nothing to help resolve her traffic ticket. I still could not believe that she had a warrant for her arrest! Thankfully, my civil attorney was able to act and get the warrants removed. What was one more outlandish attorney's bill when I had so many to pay?

Money was tight. Eating out or going to get a Coke just because were things I could no longer do. Every penny was accounted for the day I got my monthly paycheck.

Chapter 30

BETRAYALS

STORAGE UNIT (NOVEMBER 2006)

Bruce kept telling Karen that he was living in his car because he had no money; therefore, he certainly did not have money to pay for a storage unit for his possessions. As mad as I was with Bruce, I still did not want the family to lose heirlooms I knew were precious to Karen and Bruce's family.

Karen convinced Mike and Kay to see what sentimental things they wanted from our house. I knew many of the things we had in our home were from their relatives from years past since Bruce had enjoyed telling me about the history of many pieces. Some of the exquisite pieces were in Bruce's house the day I first met him in high school.

Mike agreed to pay for storage until we divided things legally. I had not seen Mike and Kay since our wedding, when she had walked into the church with the scowl she blamed on a migraine. This was going to be awkward. I dreaded seeing both of them. When I opened the door to greet them, I knew immediately that they were as nervous and uncomfortable as I was.

Kay started, "Becca, we are truly so sorry. Bruce did a wonderful job convincing us that you knew everything and you still wanted to marry him. None of this should have ever happened to you."

Their words softened the blow, but I was still hurt they hadn't warned me. I tried to just breathe, but I wanted answers. How had they come to our wedding, watched Bruce put a beautiful bracelet on my daughter's arm, knowing he had been dating his first wife secretly while he was dating me and engaged to both of us? They should have told me.

"Sorry."

I heard the sincerity in their voices, realizing they had been scammed too. I calmly accepted their help in paying for storage since I really wasn't sure of another option. I felt like I owed it to Karen and Pam. They'd been there for me. I would make sure their heirlooms were stored safely until it was decided by the courts. My trust didn't go as far as believing Mike would follow through on paying for the storage just because he told me he would. I couldn't really trust anyone at that point, but I had no choice.

Mike and Kay shared a few of the frustrations they had experienced while dealing with Bruce over the years. Mike told me, "He was not responsible with his money, so he often 'borrowed' from Mother without anyone in the family knowing." He used air quotes to show we all know it wasn't borrowing. He'd stolen it from his mother. "He shut down his business quite some time ago because he was taking care of Mother, which was just an excuse to not work. He always had an excuse for what he did."

It hadn't occurred to me that Bruce wasn't working until Detective Sheets told me Bruce's computer business was inactive with the tax office, which explained why he never billed our friends who asked him to work on their computers. An uneasy feeling grew, knowing he'd had access to my mother's computer and several of our friends' as well. What information did he steal from them? He'd always been happy to help them, but it did seem suspicious in hindsight that he'd never billed them.

It also explained why he'd *forgotten* to include our Sunday school friends' professions in the roster he created. His profession wasn't computer networking. His job was telling one lie after another and stealing from other people. His entire life was a huge lie. Our marriage was nothing but a lie.

Chapter 31

MOVING OUT

ONE DAY WOULD SEEM to stretch on endlessly, while the next would pass in a flash. Some days I would be overwhelmed with emotions, and on others, I felt nothing at all. I was just going through the motions of life, operating on autopilot until the sweetest people walked into my life.

Offer from the Stellers

Lauren and I were humbled when a generous and loving couple, Bill and Joan Stellers, offered two bedrooms for us to use as long as we needed. They were people from our church and were truly another example of Jesus working through others. I didn't know them well at the time but now consider them family. Their generosity was above and beyond what I had ever experienced from people I really didn't know. We started to make plans to move into their house and use two bedrooms. That meant that Lauren would have a room of her own again.

Barn for Storage

One of my precious friends, Sherrie Camp, called me unexpectedly. I answered anxiously, wanting to just hug her through the phone. I was not at all expecting her to make such an extraordinary offer.

She was crying when she asked, "Can we talk? I have an offer for you."

My heart skipped a beat. "Okay? You have me curious."

Sherrie empathetically sighed, "I can only imagine what you're going through right now. You know I'm here for you in any way you need."

I nodded, hoping she'd get to the point. I could tell by the way she was acting it was something big.

"You have a big house full of things that need to go somewhere. I have the barn, you know. Why don't you store your things there until things settle down?"

I blinked away tears of gratitude. "Oh, Sherrie, that is too generous. I don't have two pennies to rub together to pay you."

I could hear her smile through the phone. "You don't need to pay me anything. I just have this big old space, and it seems like you need that right now. It just makes sense, Becca."

I was humbled and blessed to have friends like Sherrie looking out for me. With her offer, I was able to store everything from our 4,800-square-foot home. Once the divorce was final, I planned on selling most of the items to help pay legal fees. I thanked God for Sherrie and for Jesus bringing her into my life when I needed her the most.

Time to Move

Later that week, my phone rang, and I glanced at the screen. It was Dillon from the bank. He was calling almost daily, but to my relief, now with a pleasant but businesslike tone. I answered, tamping down the urge to panic.

"Becca, this is Dillon. How are you holding up?"

His voice took me back to his first terrifying call when everything came tumbling down. "I'm good. I have a group of friends helping me get more things out of the house this weekend."

"That is what I'm calling about." He sounded relieved. "It will be helpful to get everything out of there so the realtor can put it on the market. The sooner the better."

"I understand. Thank you, Dillon, for everything you're doing to help." I imagined him sitting back in his office chair, less anxious about my end of things. "So many people heard our story and wanted to help."

"I'm glad your community is pulling together to help you. Selling the house will put you in a much better financial position. I'm pleased to hear you are taking steps to complete that process."

I hung up and closed my office door, needing a minute to get my composure. The entire process was emotionally and physically draining. Just two more days until we could purge our belongings from the house that had become such a nightmare.

That weekend everything came together so smoothly. I don't remember collecting boxes, tape, or packing paper. Friends took over. It was all a blur. Our neighbors grilled hamburgers for everyone's lunch as they worked. It was overwhelming and heartwarming to see the outpouring of support from my community, including folks I had never met. I'm sure we were the talk of the town, but that was the least of my concerns.

Lauren and a carload of her classmates walked in the front door as I was packing the dishes. Seeing her expression, a blanket of sorrow and guilt covered me. It was the first time Lauren had been back in the house since everything came crashing down around us. My legs shook like a newborn colt's as I ran to her and folded her in a hug. We sat in the middle of the kitchen floor, holding onto each other, tears streaming down our faces, unaware of time or the crowd around us. I wanted more than anything to take away Lauren's pain.

We'd lost everything because I fell for a despicable man. The drama with Bruce had robbed Lauren of being able to enjoy her senior year. I could not hold her tight enough or tell her I was sorry enough to change what happened. The pain and shame were a part of us now.

Packing the Closet

Later that day, the Sister Tribe and a few other close friends helped me pack up the master bedroom. I was sitting inside the closet Bruce and I once shared. My friend Leslie handed me a box filled with medicine bottles with Bruce's parents' names on them.

She asked, "What are all of these pills?"

I held up one of the bottles, eyeing the names and expiration date. "His dad died several years ago, and his mother died a month before we married." I dug deeper and found his mother's bank documents.

Leslie's eyebrows furrowed. "Why would he still have their medications when they're both gone?"

I had no answers for her. So much of how Bruce had conducted himself was a mystery to me. I couldn't fathom living the lie he had over the time I'd known him. Someone thought of checking the attic and found a few more items. I was shocked to find boxes and boxes full of unopened bills he'd saved for years. Why keep all of this? I felt like we were trapped in a mystery movie with disturbing clues revealed as the story unfolded. Yet this was no movie. It was my life.

Dining Room Tables

I finally got the credit card statements in the mail that Detective Sheets prompted me to get. My hands shook as I opened them, afraid of what I might find. I was already underwater with my finances. Sending a silent prayer there would be no more surprises, I unfolded the bill. There were several items listed there that I knew I could not afford. Desperately I wanted to avoid bankruptcy. I called the furniture store where we had purchased our dining room and kitchen tables, asking to speak to the saleslady who helped us that day. She came on the line with a stern and cold voice, unlike her earlier friendly and bubbly demeanor.

"Mrs. Walker, your husband wrote a hot check to pay for one of the tables you purchased that day. He used a credit card to purchase the other one. We no longer will be doing business with you two."

Humbled and embarrassed, I tried to spit out the words. "But, ma'am, please accept my deepest apologies. I had no idea—"

The saleslady interjected, "Ma'am, I don't need your apology. We need the table you purchased with the hot check. I'll send someone to pick it up in the morning. Goodbye."

Click.

I'd never had a salesperson speak to me like that. Being humiliated was the least of my worries.

A light bulb turned on, realizing why Bruce had asked me to go to the car to cool down—so I'd not be around when he used my old credit card. The following day the store came to collect our furniture. Another business repossessed the new refrigerator purchased with one of my other reactivated credit cards. What a fool I had been to trust Bruce! I should have shredded the credit cards, rather than taking his advice to keep them "just in case" someone ever asked about them.

My pride was demolished. I simply tried not to focus on the overwhelming embarrassment of what was happening. Just one more humiliation thrust upon me by my husband's misdeeds.

Chapter 32

OPENING THE TRUTH

THE STELLERS' BEAUTIFUL AND loving home was around the corner from our (once upon a time) dream home. I frequently found myself driving to the vacant house, realizing it was an empty shell. It had never been our warm and welcoming home.

The Stellers' generosity was more than just rooms in their house. Because they wanted us to feel totally comfortable in their home, they moved their guest room furniture into a storage unit and allowed Lauren to make her own space by moving her bedroom furniture and belongings in there. Lauren was finally able to sleep in her own bed and feel safe.

Only a child of God would go to such lengths to help their guests feel more at home. They went above and beyond making us feel welcome with their sweet hospitality. They constantly reassured us their home was our home for as long as we needed it. They were a gift from Jesus.

Unopened Mail

The first Saturday morning we lived with the Stellers, I covered their formal dining room table with boxes of Bruce's unopened mail someone had thought to recover from the dream home's attic. These boxes held the financial papers from Bruce and his mother, an ominous symbol of Bruce's irresponsibility and lies. As Joan and I opened each envelope, we put one more piece of the puzzle together.

I came across the paperwork that revealed Bruce's mother had purchased the house he was living in on the day of the yard sale when I first visited him. Bruce had told me he sold the house in one day. Another lie. The truth is he did not sell the house at all. He lost it because the bank foreclosed on the property. His mother must have known this the day I dropped by, and she was helping pack his china. Or was her corrupt son able to lie his way out of it once again to stay in her good graces? I wished June was around to tell me herself.

We also learned there were liens placed on his mother's farms. His brothers blamed Bruce for mismanaging their mother's funds, and the paperwork confirmed this. This is why Bruce only chose a few "sentimental things" from his mother's estate while his brothers loaded furs, large pieces of furniture, china, and crystal after her death. This matched what Mike had explained to me when they came to the house.

I will never forget when Bruce whispered to me, "Becca, I would really like to move up our wedding date. There's no reason to wait until the summer. Don't you agree?"

The excitement of starting a new life with him was all I had dreamed about. I wish I'd known the truth. When his mother died, her funds were no longer available to abuse, therefore it was essential to marry me sooner. Almost two years later I sat stunned, drained, and numb as I read through the mounds of paperwork divulging irresponsible and corrupt business dealings. This also explained why Bruce kept driving a wedge between his brothers and me, throwing doubt on their character. He didn't want us getting closer where they may reveal the truth about his shady behavior.

The clock struck 2:30 in the wee hours of the morning. Joan and I had once again found ourselves staying up way too late while opening envelopes and trying to put a few pieces of the puzzle together. Sweet Bill surprised us with a plate of cookies as he yawned and asked, "When do y'all ever sleep?"

I grabbed a cookie and answered, "I know, I'm tired. I'm exhausted, but I think I just realized something new. Bruce had insisted that Lauren and I were to start a home theater business in my name. He was excited about the name of it being something that we would agree upon. His only involvement would be having his men do the work. He told me that it would be a great business for me if I ever got to where I couldn't work physically and do the job I was doing." I smirked sarcastically, "Wasn't he kind and thoughtful, always thinking of me?"

Hindsight is twenty-twenty, but living with a sociopath keeps you blindsided. It all became clear to me at Joan's table; Bruce insisted the home theater business would be in my name because his credit was already ruined. However, it was only a temporary fix, since he quickly ruined my good credit. What was his plan?

New York City Trip Farce

A few days later, when I'd regained strength to face more trouble, I decided to find out the truth about the promised trip to New York City for the Macy's Day Parade. I went to the travel agency Bruce had mentioned. This time I was expecting something sinister, and it hurt a little less.

When I asked for the woman who had helped Bruce, the receptionist looked at me blankly. "I'm sorry, ma'am. We don't have anyone here by that name."

"Maybe I have the name wrong. Can you look up our account?"

She obliged, but after a few minutes of gathering information, she blinked at me, dumbfounded. "I'm sorry. I can't find him anywhere in our system. He's not in here." She tapped the screen with a long-glossed fingernail. "We've never done business with your husband."

I was quick to respond as I spewed, "Oh, he's not one I would consider as husband material. He's a heartless imitation."

Another of Bruce's lies. He'd just spit out a fictitious name when I'd asked about it. I walked out of the travel agency and sat on the curb lifeless.

Why did he tell me he bought these tickets last summer? He'd even gone so far as to promise my eighty-year-old mother a room with the view facing the parade. He'd built up Lauren's hopes, only for disappointment. Why all the lies? The sad truth hit me in the face; I had already known it. Bruce never loved us. He'd only used us to get his cruel laughs. Betraying us had become a sick form of entertainment for his twisted mind. It was all a game to him, and we were his pawns. He was simply diabolical!

Chapter 33

BRUCE'S DECEIT RAN DEEP

IT WAS DIFFICULT TO understand how many people Bruce lied to—perhaps everyone he'd ever met. He certainly knew how to keep me in the dark. He purposefully kept me from getting close to his brothers and their wives by planting seeds of doubt about their character. My health issues were used as a wedge between the builder and contractors. The bankers were warned I was too sick to be contacted all the while he was providing false documents to show *my* funds would pay for our new home.

Bruce fabricated everything: what he'd inherited from his mother's passing and, most insidious, how our home was *dedicated to the Lord*. How was he capable of being deceitful to so many people, then quote scripture, and feel NO remorse? But then, Satan knows scripture too, doesn't he?

I realize now Bruce exploited my faith, manipulating me with the pretense of being a good Christian man. He knew precisely how important my faith was and became the person to fulfill my needs. Bruce used God and Biblical scriptures to help me fall in love with him, but he never loved me at all. He only loved himself and the game he played to cheat and win with NO remorse.

Where was the man who prayed the most beautiful prayers and shared, without hesitation, his favorite Bible verses? The words he spoke as he proposed tore through me:

"Now we see but a poor reflection as in a mirror; then we shall see face to face. Now I know in part; then I shall know fully, even as I am fully known. And now these three remain: faith, hope, and love; but the greatest of these is love" (1 Corinthians 13:12-13 CSB).

Those words hit me hard, and I covered my mouth, shocked at this revelation. Bruce was unable to hide his deceptive character from God, yet he asked for my hand by claiming "even as I am fully known." The three promises of faith, love, and hope were nothing more than his lies. Now, all that remained was faith. *My faith.*

Scripture warns us:

Enemies disguise themselves with their lips, but in their hearts they harbor deceit. Though their speech is charming, do not believe them, for seven abominations fill their hearts. Their malice may be concealed by deception, but their wickedness will be exposed in the assembly. Whoever digs a pit will fall into it; if someone rolls a stone, it will roll back on them. A lying tongue hates those it hurts, and a flattering mouth works ruin (Proverbs 26:24-25 NIV).

Proof of Forgery

One sleepless night I decided to open one more box I'd found in the attic of our dream house. Inside was a ream of white paper. When I lifted the first blank page, I was puzzled when I found writing in the center of each page in the same black pen. Some sheets had only one name, where others had several names. Most of them were written in cursive.

It hit me all at once. These were Bruce's practice sheets for forging signatures. I felt dirty just touching those papers. It made my skin crawl knowing he'd sat somewhere in my house practicing his crimes. The next morning, I delivered the box to Detective Sheets, hoping they could help others who'd been a victim of Bruce's criminal activity. I was incredibly relieved to get that box out of my car.

I was stressed, exhausted, and distraught. Every nerve in my body was working overtime with the constant surprises in the aftermath of being married to such a relentlessly sick man. It was hard for me to accept that we'd been living with a lying con man for eighteen months.

How thankful I am for the Lord's words where Scripture tells us:

The Lord is my rock, my fortress, and my Savior; my God is my rock, in whom I find protection. He is my shield, the power that saves me, and my place of safety. He is my refuge, my Savior, the one who saves me from violence. I called on the Lord, who is worthy of praise, and He saved me from my enemies (2 Samuel 22: 1-4 NL T).

The Secret Duplex

Trying to get answers, I left work early and drove to the electric company, asking what address or post office box our bill was mailed to every month. I certainly did not have a key to our post office box to see any bills.

The lady behind the counter looked at her computer and asked, "Which meter were you referring to?"

I was floored. "How many are there?"

She glanced at the computer, then tentatively told me, "Two."

Fearfully I asked, "Ma'am, is one attached to the house we live in and the second meter possibly for the pool house?"

She studied the computer screen closely, then her eyes narrowed. "You're not on the account. I'm not authorized to share any more information about this."

My knees shook. This was almost word for word what they told me at the post office.

As I explained my frustration with Bruce to the lady behind the counter, I was clearly upset. Another lady walked me to a private office and brought me a bottle of water and a box of Kleenex. Her supervisor came in to console me, but they were not legally allowed to let me know the address of the second meter. I pleaded with her.

Detective Sheets later verified that the second meter was for the duplex Bruce had rented before we married and continued to rent without my knowledge for almost eighteen months. Once Bruce moved out of our home, he moved back to his duplex. Surely he knew I'd find out about the duplex. He claimed he was living out of his car. I wondered if he EVER spoke the truth about anything.

I'd thought I'd reached the lowest point in this life lesson. Lauren and I were not prepared for what we next uncovered. Bruce's deception was deeper than any of us could have anticipated.

Chapter 34

THANKSGIVING SURPRISE

THERE HAVE BEEN MANY Thanksgivings come and go in my lifetime but never like the last one with Bruce. The morning of Thanksgiving, Lauren and I set out to drive to my sister's for the weekend to enjoy a holiday meal with family and a much-needed reprieve from our nightmare.

I hadn't planned on a detour to Bruce's secret duplex and was surprised to find myself pulling up to the driveway to see if he was there before we left town. My heart was beating in my throat, and beads of sweat poured off my forehead. Part of me hoped he was not there so we could go on our merry way. I was not so lucky.

His SUV was backed up to the open garage door, and to my utter shock, I recognized several of my grandmother's paintings and lamps leaning up against a wall. This ignited my anger from head to toe. The very idea of my family heirlooms near him sickened me. Those were my deceased grandmother's things! He had no right to keep them, much less stash them in his secret lair. The last time I'd seen these precious keepsakes, they were in our shared storage unit. We'd kept planning on taking them out when we moved into our dream house, but Bruce always made excuses that he was too busy being the "general contractor" for the dream house. What else had he stolen from us?

My blood was boiling as I pulled into the driveway. As I got closer, I could see many of our office totes stacked up along the walls. It was clear now why he did not want our files in a filing cabinet! The large totes made it easier to move everything to HIS duplex! I wanted to kick, hit, and scream at his violation. The totes were full of business papers I had been searching for over the last month. I couldn't just drive away and pretend this wasn't happening. I called my sister Caitlin and asked her to listen to my altercation with Bruce. I wanted her as a witness.

When Bruce realized Lauren and I were there, he stepped into view, walking through the garage toward us, blinking rapidly as if we'd startled him. His hands remained in his oversized jacket pockets. At the time I wasn't sure if he had a weapon, but my rage made me confront him anyway.

"Why do you have my grandmother's things in there?" My voice was high as I barked out each word. "I'm not the first you have done this to. I know you stole from your own mother!"

He stared at me emotionlessly, as if my words meant nothing to him. This enraged me even more.

"Don't stand there and act like a saint. There was filth on all the computers!"

While I railed at him, the stony indifference shifted to a sly, creepy smile. He was reveling in how he'd made me lose my composure. Where was that sweet man I'd known, the one who had a calming answer for all my life's problems? That man was long gone, replaced with a conniving, wicked, and wholly unrecognizable shell.

I continued, determined to say everything I'd bottled up for so long. "Obviously you are addicted to porn. How can you pretend to be such a good *Christian* man! Do you actually think I'd never find out about Anne? What possesses a person to sink so low as to lie to two women about the sacred vow of marriage? You are pathetic!"

Lauren sat in the car looking shell-shocked. She'd never heard me roar like a tiger before.

Bruce pasted on a smile that didn't reach his eyes as he calmly condescended to my outburst, the tone in contrast to my frenetic words. "Becca, there is nothing to get upset about." His words came across as vile, cold-hearted, with the intention of putting me in my place. He enjoyed patronizing me as if *he* were the logical, mature party in all of this.

I had a lot more to say to him, and I continued unfazed. "You stole my good credit! You paid twenty-one months of rent for your secret duplex at $800 a month? No, I retract that. I basically paid $17,000 in rent for your secret duplex. WHY?" When he didn't answer, I added, "There was a reason God never made you a father."

Adrenaline surged through me, but I was tired of being his victim. I was sure he was going to pull out a gun or grab me. He was acting strange, laughing under his breath, and rolling his eyes, but his hands remained in his pockets. He must have been on drugs because he was acting nothing like when we were married.

At this point, Lauren's scared voice carried through the garage from the car window. "Mom, he's not worth it."

Undeterred, I grabbed my grandmother's paintings, lamps, and anything I could grab, all the while expecting him to stop me. I knew I would never have another chance.

Lauren surprised me as I loaded the trunk with the last remaining items. She yelled to Bruce, "I just want you to know that you tore my heart to pieces. I thought you were a good man who could be trusted." Bruce tried to respond, but Lauren didn't give him a chance. "No, you don't get to talk. You will listen to me! My mom didn't deserve this. We've been through so many hard times. She is a great person. I hope you know what you are missing." Then she rolled her window up, closing the conversation by turning away from him, not allowing him to respond.

I opened the driver's side door, turning toward him. "YOU are despicable! I thought you were a Christian, but now I know you don't have a clue who Jesus is. The sad thing is you have to live with yourself. Thankfully, we no longer have to." I slammed the door and locked it, a trickle of sweat pouring off me.

Bruce stepped closer to the car, watching us pull out of the driveway. I was shocked to hear wicked laughter following us as I stole a glance back at him. That pure evil laugh burned in my mind forever.

I turned to Lauren. "God, help us! Let's get out of here!" My body was shaking with fury. I had not planned to see him or say anything to him at all, but when I saw the garage door open and MY things inside, I couldn't help but spill out the pent-up rage that had been building for months now. It was the spark rising into a wildfire. Later I learned that he had a recording device in his pocket when my attorney received a handwritten note from him with every word I had said, making me seem unhinged.

We drove an hour to Caitlin's house, shell-shocked. My body was still trembling as I fell into her arms. She held me just like she had when we were little girls and our house was burning to the ground.

Thanksgiving was normally a day of reflecting on blessings, family, and friends. I was unnerved by the sickening surprises we'd encountered at Bruce's. That morning had been a shock to my system. Somehow, some way, with God's help, we were able to settle into an afternoon filled with family, a wonderful meal, and moments of reprieve. We thanked God for our many blessings. Lauren and I were alive and blessed to have each other. We couldn't hug each other enough throughout the day. Feeling the peace that only comes from Jesus, in all circumstances, was a gift I appreciated more than ever.

Lauren and I shared a bed in my sister's guest room that night. It wasn't uncommon for us to talk until the wee hours of the night, but I was exhausted and fell asleep before my head hit the pillow. God had given me the strength to confront Bruce and recover a few cherished items. I tried not to dwell on the difficulty of disentangling our lives from Bruce. There was still so much to do.

Chapter 35

DISCONNECTING FROM BRUCE

WHEN LOOKING BACK, I realize how many pieces of the puzzle were hidden from me. Detective Sheets dug deeper and learned that Bruce continued to use my name for false collateral. The duplex Bruce rented and lived in after he *sold* his house was only rented. However, a background check revealed that he and I owned the duplex he rented. We never did own it! It was just another lie with my name attached.

Cell Phone

Realizing my cell phone bill was out of control, I skirted into the store looking for the friendliest face.

"Ma'am, I am in a little bit of a pickle. My cell phone bill has increased tremendously this last month, and I need to know why. Can you help me?"

"Let me just look a moment at your account." She clicked on the keyboard for a minute as she pulled up my information. "Oh yes, the number that was recently added to the account has some internet charges that increased your last statement."

"What number has been added without my knowledge, ma'am?"

She confirmed that Bruce had added his number to my bill, and that the internet charges were mainly from the middle of the night. Her eyebrows rose when she chose not to say another word. My face was flushed from embarrassment, knowing probably from his vile addictions.

It clearly was a game for Bruce. I imagined him rubbing his hands together like a cartoon villain, scheming for new ways to take my money and my peace of mind, hiding puzzle pieces from my reach. I was incensed. I immediately called Mr. Phillips. I hoped he would be just as alarmed and agree that I needed to take Bruce's number off my account.

"Becca, unfortunately, if we disconnect his phone, we may not have a way of reaching Bruce. I encourage you to leave it as is for the time being."

I couldn't believe it. Bruce won again! I was paying dearly for his deplorable, sick habits. SO...I continued to pay for his phone and kept it in my contract. I don't remember how many months it was before I could turn off his phone, but my Sister Tribe was there with me the day I was able to discontinue his service, rejoicing in one small victory.

Wedding Ring

One day I realized my bank account was as dry as the desert. I had to talk to my attorney to see what options I had.

I swallowed my pride and called. "Mr. Phillips, it's Becca again. To be very blunt, I am running low on funds. I'm hoping to sell a few things I know neither Bruce nor I will ever need. One item is my wedding ring." It felt like I was asking my daddy for an advancement with my allowance.

"Becca, I would advise you not to sell anything until the courts decide. Bruce could come back and accuse you of fraud."

That shocked me. He could accuse me of fraud after all the devious things he's gotten away with?

I pled my case. "But, Mr. Phillips, my wedding ring was a gift, not communal property."

"Please, Becca. I understand your situation, but as your attorney, I advise you to hold off on selling anything until we have this all settled."

After a great deal of research, I decided to sell it for $1,300, which immediately paid for a small amount of my legal fees.

Safety Deposit Box

My cell phone rang, as it often did at work, with either the bank's personnel, my attorney's office, or Detective Sheets. Strangely, this seemed like a new circle of friends since I talked to them more often than anyone else.

"Becca, do you have a minute?" Sheets asked.

"What's up this time?" I cringed, not wanting to hear any more upsetting news.

"I hate to tell you this, but Bruce set up a safety deposit box using your account at the Whisper Creek National Bank. You have an account with them here in town."

"Okay?" I held my breath as she continued. It had been my regular bank when Lauren and I lived on the other side of town many years ago, but since then we'd moved, I changed banks, leaving only a small amount in an account. I had almost forgotten about it.

She prodded. "So, you were unaware of the safety deposit box, Becca?"

Bruce must have found the folder with the banking information while he lurked in my filing cabinet, finding one more opportunity to use me. "It's just another one of Bruce's surprises. I'll go tomorrow and confirm what I already know...that my name is not on the account."

The next day I found my way to the bank, knowing it was likely a waste of time. Mrs. Cunningham, a redheaded lady wearing high heels, met me in the lobby of the Whisper Creek National Bank with a friendly smile.

Compassion oozed off of her. She must have read my tired and distraught face as I explained why I was there. "I'm sorry. I can't use your marriage license to access the safety deposit box." She escorted me to a hall of offices to confirm this with someone else who was not prepared for my mysterious safety deposit box story. A Mr. Bowen smiled formally at me and offered a seat in his tidy office.

I braced myself for a hard no. "Hello, my name is Becca Walker. I have had a checking and savings account with you for several years. I closed out the savings account completely years ago when I moved across town but left a small amount in the checking account. I was told today that I also have a safety deposit box I didn't know about. Would you confirm that please?"

Mr. Bowen took down all my information, scanned my driver's license, and looked at the computer screen with skeptical eyes.

He pressed his lips together, cautiously eyeing me. "Ma'am, your name is not on the safety deposit box, therefore I cannot discuss the matter with you."

"So what you are telling me in so many words is someone, without my knowledge, has authorized access to a safety deposit box using my checking account? He signed up without authorization?"

Mr. Bowen sat back in his chair. "Ma'am, I am sorry, but I cannot discuss the matter with you."

I couldn't decide if I should laugh or cry. It felt like a rerun. Another account without my name on it, without my authorization or access to it. Had he brought a female with him to pretend to be me when he opened the safety deposit box? How many more keys of deception would I discover?

Later I learned he had stored his father's coin collection in that safety deposit box and sold it to an old friend by telling him an emotional and believable story, then walked away with $20,000 from that "dear friend."

Chapter 36

THE VICTIM

MAXED OUT

When I had my credit checked, a report came back confirming Bruce had changed the mailing address for all four of my credit cards. He likely reached the spending limits on all of them, further ruining my good credit. I never felt so ignorant as I did then. Those cards had been my security blanket long before I found Bruce, knowing they were there in case of an emergency. The day he convinced me to keep them is scorched in my brain. Why did I trust him so completely? I have always looked for the best in people and had no reason to be suspicious of anyone, especially not someone I'd married. I'd never known someone capable of appearing so genuinely loving but living a life full of corruption and deceit.

My instructions were to call the credit card companies and change the address back to my new one. I locked myself in my office to make necessary phone calls, after letting my boss know what had happened. My hands shook as I took notes to prepare for the calls. This was insane! How was I going to convince these people the credit cards were mine? It felt like an almost impossible task over the phone.

The first company I called sent me to their supervisor. After I gave her my account numbers, I explained my situation. "My credit report showed this card has been reactivated without my knowledge. My current balance shows I owe $14,000. I opened the account over ten years ago but have rarely used it. This must be a mistake because I've not used this card in years."

A lady with a thick accent asked, "Ma'am, may I get a little information please? Your date of birth? Your mailing address? What is the password? Your phone number? Ma'am, these are not matching up. I will need to send you to another department."

"But what's not matching up? This is my account, and this is my information. Before you transfer me, can you please give me your name and number for my notes?"

"My name is Miriam, and I don't have a number. My line was open, so I answered. The next time it may be someone else."

"Okay, thank you."

After waiting on hold for nearly ten minutes, a man came on the line. "Ma'am, I understand that you have already answered many questions, but I am required to gather as much information as I can if we go any further." My blood was boiling too much to concentrate on anything but getting this resolved.

Once again, I asked for his name and number in case we were disconnected, then got to the point. "Sir, my husband, Bruce Walker, used my name to reactivate my account without my authorization. Passwords, telephone numbers, and addresses have all been changed without my knowledge. I am working with a fraud detective and am slowly putting pieces together. Please, will you help me?"

He paused for a second and my heart sank. "Ma'am, I'm sorry, I don't have the authorization to go any further. I'll need to send you to someone who maybe can help you."

He must have heard the emotion in my voice. "But sir, I've been on the phone for over an hour and talked to three people. I'm being treated like I'm trying to defraud you. I have not used this card in years. My husband is to blame, and I need to report these charges as fraud."

"I understand. I will need to send you to another department, ma'am. I'm sure they can help you."

Before I could say a word, I was transferred. The music in the background was calming, yet my heart beat twice as fast and my foot wouldn't quit tapping the floor. After twenty minutes on hold, the phone disconnected. I spent half the afternoon on the phone with nothing to show for my time.

I wondered how Bruce changed the information. Did he have a female accomplice who helped reactivate my cards? Or did he manipulate computer keys to steal my cards online? He was brilliantly dishonest.

After days of calling each credit card customer service department, I finally started throwing out Bruce's phone number. Something was different on the other line. I could tell that after they heard what I had been through they might finally believe me.

A lady who had taken almost thirty minutes of her time listening finally said my phone number had been changed. The last digit was different. Later I learned that Bruce had changed that one digit on all the credit card accounts he had reactivated and none of my passwords were correct anymore.

By June, my credit card balances were close to $60,000. At the time, I was woefully oblivious to any of these fraudulent charges. Because they were all maxed out, I had no way of paying for them. I knew I was going to be forced to file for bankruptcy after the divorce was final, but until then, I was advised to make the minimum payments.

There were months I just couldn't afford to, but life went on. My body went through the motions sometimes of just existing, but every morning the sun would rise and shine.

Bruce's Cunning Fraud

When Bruce set up our home loan, he'd used Natural Falls State Bank, where Dillon worked, and Falls State Mortgage, who was affiliated with the bank. Before offering the loan, they'd done a pathetic job researching our financial status. On top of that, Bruce had convinced them to leave me out of all business matters. He told them I was in poor health and had an extremely stressful job. They followed his wishes, willingly keeping me out of the loop as long as possible. After the truth was known, I'm not sure who felt the most foolish, them or me. Bruce was a sociopath king who knew how to play the game so well he fooled a banker and a mortgage lende r.

When I spoke to my divorce attorney, Harold Phillips, it was always to the point, probably because he knew I didn't have the money for long conversations and he had a busy schedule.

I called him to follow up on some details we'd been working on. "Mr. Phillips, hello. Because Bruce is representing himself rather than using an attorney, it bothers me that he is calling you and I am having to pay for those conversations."

"Becca, it may sound odd, but if he were using an attorney, I would bill you for the time we spoke. The same applies for Bruce representing himself."

"I understand. I just wanted to warn you about the mind games he plays. I know he loves the thought of racking up a large attorney's bill and sticking me with more debt."

Mr. Phillips cleared his throat. "I certainly am taking that into account, Becca, and I assure you I am going to be cutting my conversations with him short."

I had faith in him, an experienced divorce attorney, and thought he would be wise to manipulating spouses, but Bruce was at another level. The time Bruce pretended to be his brother when he was being served divorce papers rushed through my mind.

We spoke for some time discussing the case until he said something shocking. "Becca, on another note, we need to work with the bank as closely as we can. They are in essence the victim and we need to keep in constant communication with them. I know you have been left out of the loop regarding the building process, but they are going to lean on you, not Bruce, to finish the house so they can sell and get their money back as quickly as possible."

I was stuck on his words, not processing the rest of what he had said. How was the *bank* the victim? Wasn't *I* the victim? I stared out my office window in disbelief. I could not breathe. "The *bank* is the victim? What about me? Bruce stole $45,000, basically my entire life savings. He took every penny in my daughter's bank account, reactivated my credit cards, then maxed out and defaulted on them. He created false collateral in my name, abused and ruined my good credit, forced me to file for bankruptcy and foreclose on the house. But yet I was not the victim—the bank was?"

Mr. Phillips, to his credit, was very patient, carefully explaining, "As difficult as it is to digest, the bank leant you both the money to build the house. The mortgage company has the biggest loss, the enormous loan on the house."

"I don't understand. They have the house as collateral. They will get their money back when it sells. When do I get reimbursed for everything he's taken from me?"

I had nothing left. We were homeless, penniless, and the bank would carry on, with a small bump in the road.

"For goodness sake, Mr. Phillips. I didn't even want to spend so much on this big, fancy house. Now I am strapped with bankruptcy. I've lost everything. Can you tell me this? How did both the mortgage company and the bank fall for not one, but three of Bruce's fake money market accounts, allow him to forge signatures, kite checks, and rack up enormous bills? It was the bank who failed by not thoroughly researching our finances before lending us the money. They had every tool available to protect their investment. The consequences were enormous for me with the destruction of my financial and personal life. After all, they lent money to a *known con artist*, one who had been in jail twice for writing hot checks and putting up false collateral to borrow against my good credit. What was their excuse for falling for his scams? They're all trained to sniff out financial fraudsters. I was physically sick, trying to raise my daughter and just cope with life."

Mr. Phillips was silent as I continued my rant.

"Bruce didn't even have a real job for most of the time we were together. Why hadn't they performed a simple background check where they would have seen his criminal record for writing hot checks? Certainly they would have refused the loan. Even if they somehow gave it to us because of *my* credit, shouldn't they have made sure I was heavily involved in all the finances to be sure he wasn't taking advantage of me like he had other people?"

Mr. Phillips was quick to insert, "The bank has measures in place to protect their loans, I'm sure. I don't know the ins and outs of it. This is not my area of expertise."

I could only shake my head, trying to make sense of any of this. "So, I'm just stuck with the mess to clean up, to pay for expensive legal bills for divorce and civil attorneys, filing for bankruptcy, forcing my daughter to suffer through homelessness while we are completely dependent on the charity of our friends? All because Bruce played the game like a pro. If they'd only done their job, it would have alerted me to Bruce's real nature before he'd ruined our lives."

I don't think he knew what to say to me. Any sane person would see this was Bruce's fraud. He should be punished, and I should be made whole from his criminal behavior. This was a dose of cruel injustice to swallow. I felt victimized by the bank as well as by Bruce.

Two days passed and I remember walking, yet I had no idea my feet were even moving. It was like my head and the rest of my body were detached. I simply was surviving.

I whispered, "Sweet Jesus, you're going to have to carry me. I can't take much more."

Chapter 37

A HOME AT LAST

DECEMBER 2006

Bill and Joan had made it clear we were welcome to live in their home as long as we needed. Their extreme generosity was genuine. I certainly saw Jesus in their eyes. They made their home our home.

My heart ached to the core knowing it was Lauren's last Christmas before graduating high school. I wanted more than anything to give her a Christmas in our own home with our ornaments on the tree. Every year before Bruce showed up, we had a sweet, simple home we loved. Our Christmas tree ornaments and decorations we had enjoyed collecting during Lauren's childhood were gone. The man I thought once loved us had no intentions to give me any of our sentimental items he had put in storage.

One night I woke up repeatedly with intense anxiety, sweating as I imagined Lauren's last Christmas before she graduated missing all the special touches to celebrate our Lord and Savior we'd always enjoyed. It broke my heart I couldn't continue our traditions because I'd trusted the wrong man.

Soon after, I got an unexpected call from our Sunday school class friend, Claire. She cheerfully asked, "Can you and Lauren come to class this Sunday?"

Surprised, I stammered, "Excuse me, this Sunday...Lauren and me?"

Claire responded, "Yes, our class has something we would like to give you both, and it would be very special if you could be there."

I was touched knowing we had people out there thinking of us.

I eagerly replied, "Absolutely! We look forward to being there." Bruce and I had been active in our church and Sunday school, enjoying their fellowship. It was a lifetime ago when everyone had loved Bruce, who had been a quiet listener and friend. Now everything had changed; the truth about Bruce was well known.

Sunday came and we drove to the church, curious about what Claire had in store for us. The sun was shining, and the day felt full of promise. Months ago, the sun may have been shining but I wouldn't have noticed. The simple things in life became so much more important throughout this struggle. We rolled down the windows and inhaled the fresh air, happy to focus on the weather without a penny to our name.

Lauren and I stumbled into the room as many friends smiled and gave us hugs from the heart. Hugs that were not gentle but hugs that were full of love, that helped us know their love was genuine. It was real.

Claire and her husband hushed the room and spoke, looking toward me and my daughter with smiles that couldn't be wider or happier. Claire shared, "Jesus loves us all. We are His children. We are blessed to be a blessing. This morning, we choose to bless Becca and Lauren, our sisters in Christ."

Before I ever blinked an eye, Claire and the rest of the class walked over to hand us a sealed envelope. They asked if they could pray over us. As they placed their hands on us, I knew we were being blessed by Jesus. I had no idea how generous the group of friends was, but I knew we were blessed.

Lauren and I thanked each person for their hospitality and held hands as we walked to the car. It was humbling to accept their loving gift, but I knew it was an answer to prayer and from God. I waited until we were blocks away before I pulled into a parking lot and opened the envelope. As I counted each bill, my hands started to shake. Lauren and I jumped with gladness, like little girls on Christmas morning. Their generous gift allowed me to put a deposit and first month's rent on a duplex of our own. We moved in right before Christmas. God knew I wanted my daughter to have a place to call home by the holidays. I will never forget the sweet friends who made this possible. You never forget people who bless you when you are rock bottom.

After we moved into our new and humble home, my favorite part of the day was when we would sit down at the dinner table and have a meal together. I treasured this time together more than life itself. We prayed before we ate, just as we always had. I savored every minute, because it gave me a sense of normalcy in the midst of the storm. It didn't matter how simple the meal was. It was our time together that mattered. We talked about anything and everything. We laughed and cried, almost like things had returned to normal, at least for a few moments. My daughter's smile was returning, and it warmed my heart. At times, my heart felt giddy.

Outside of these moments, Bruce was not far from our thoughts. In fact, he was not far from our new house either. Two weeks later, I was driving home and spotted him in his car at a stop sign one block from our house. Our eyes locked. I couldn't help but notice one of his shirts hanging in the backseat.

Our sweet elderly neighbor, Mr. Lambert, had seen Bruce drive by several times while I was at work. He later testified in court that Bruce was stalking me, recounting Bruce had sat for hours in his car in front of my duplex on more than one occasion. I installed a security system as soon as I realized he was lurking about. I knew Bruce once owned a handgun, and that kept me up many nights. Peace from Jesus was stolen at times with anxiety, but thankfully I had prayer warriors helping me feel the stability only Jesus can give.

Protective Order

I mentioned Bruce's stalking to Detective Sheets. She encouraged me to get a protective order against Bruce, which I did. I wished these measures would take away my concern for Lauren's safety, but they did not. A protective order was merely a piece of paper. Bruce wouldn't let that get in the way of whatever nefarious acts he had in mind. I had no clue what his intentions or limitations were.

Lying in bed at night, I would try to think back to when my life felt normal. Memories of when Bruce and I became reacquainted felt normal. How I wished I had known the truth about his character. Our lives would have certainly turned out differently.

A Friendship Ends

Soon after I moved into our new house, I received a letter from my dear friend Pam, Bruce's cousin. When she'd discovered Bruce's deceit, her world was shattered. She adored Bruce and loved Lauren and me. Our marriage gave her a sense of family and security, yet it was stripped away in a split second. In the letter she told me she'd gotten professional help to deal with the pain of Bruce's misdeeds. She'd made the decision to cut ties with me so she could heal. It was a final goodbye, explaining this drastic step was necessary for her mental health and asked me to please not respond in ANY way.

It was heartbreaking. Our lifelong friendship ended abruptly. In a way, it felt like Pam had died suddenly. I couldn't hug her, cry with her, or even say goodbye. As badly as I wanted to hug her with all my might at least one more time, I knew out of love I needed to respect her wishes.

As scripture reminded me, "Love is patient, love is kind. It does not envy, it does not dishonor others, it is not self-seeking, it is not easily angered, it keeps no record of wrongs" (1 Corinthians 13:4-5 N IV).

We have not spoken since. I pray for her well-being often and always will. She didn't deserve any of this hurt, yet her heart was shattered into a million pieces.

Chapter 38

PREPARING TO SELL

JANUARY 2007

The bank suggested a particular well-known and successful re-altor, Jace Kirkpatrick, to put the house on the market. I agreed to anything the bank wanted, as I prayed that we would not have to foreclose. My good credit was already ruined by the bills Bruce had racked up in my name, but I did not want a foreclosure added to the list of embarrassments. I started to work with Jace immediately.

"Becca, I hate to add any pressure to what you are already dealing with, but the beautiful swimming pool is going to help sell the house, but only if it is maintained. You need to find a way to get a cleaning service there weekly and do whatever it takes to look as pretty as it was built to be."

Taking a deep breath, I closed my eyes and was thankful we were on the phone where Jace couldn't see my fury. To sell the extrav-agant house I never really wanted, I had to spend more money I didn't have. The pool had just been finished a week earlier, and I had never even put my foot in it.

I had to find a way, so I told him, "I'll see what I can do." I was numb. I didn't have the money to pay for a pool service, so the job was mine. I didn't know anything about pools, and I didn't have any time to spare to take care of it.

Because of Jesus, I was able to cope with the present and have hope for our future. Without Jesus I would have crawled in bed and would never have moved a muscle.

Thankfully, friends recommended friends once I shared my story, and they knew something about cleaning pools. Asking for help was humbling and overwhelming. It was more complicated than I ever imagined. A notebook became my best friend as I kept track of which valve to turn left and which to turn right, what to twist off and clean, and what chemicals to use. It was one more responsibility added to my burden, but I had no choice.

From the moment I saw Bruce's forgeries and corruption, I protected myself by emotionally detaching from the new house. If I allowed myself to cry, I might not ever quit. The emptiness of the house reflected the emptiness I felt. Yes, the pool and waterfall were beautiful, but they were never mine. They were never Bruce's either. I tried to not think of the day we buried the Bible under the foundation. The house was built on lies and deception, NOT on the Word of God.

I spent two full days cleaning the dream home so the realtors could take pictures for the virtual tour. I tried to thank Jesus for my blessings, especially since I would not be living with a sociopath anymore. The second day I was sweeping the front porch, Bruce's SUV drove by, making me feel uneasy. I locked the doors and drove to a friend's house, knowing very well that he knew where I was.

When a friend of a friend showed interest in the house, I got my hopes up. I showed it to the couple without a moment's notice. It was larger than they wanted but said I should be a realtor because of the way I showed all the special features.

Landscaper's Gift

While cleaning the pool one cloudy afternoon, I was surprised to see the landscaper, Wayne Stockington. He had come to check on the yard. I'm sure the bank was asking him to come often because the landscaping Bruce had chosen was extremely expensive. His gentle spirit and genuine concern were evident when he started to speak. He was overcome with emotions and couldn't finish his first sentence. There were tears in his eyes as he finally choked out what he'd wanted to say.

"My wife and I have been praying for you and your daughter. Jesus put it on my heart to tell you something." He looked down at his feet, then looked me in the eyes. "You are about the same age as my daughter, and my grandson is close to your daughter's age, I'm guessing." He took out a handkerchief and wiped his eyes. "You and your daughter are going to need support. A great friend of mine is a Christian counselor. I would like to pay for several sessions for the both of you. Would you let me do that please?"

Pride did not keep me from taking him up on his offer, and the counselor helped us get through the aftermath of the storm. How nice it was to know in the middle of the darkness that there was light. A stranger cared enough to extend Christian love to me and Lauren.

I will never forget Mr. Stockington. Because of his compassionate and generous heart, we were able to seek wise counsel. His gift provided us with a counselor who loved the Lord, had knowledge of the scriptures, life experiences, and an expertise in counseling that paved the way for our healing to begin.

Chapter 39

WHEN WOULD IT END

FEBRUARY 2007

College Prep

There was "life" happening outside of my world. Lauren was a senior, which meant that we had to look at options for her after graduation. Thankfully, her dad and I had set up a college fund that was a huge help, one Bruce had not gotten his hands on. We had to fill out FAFSA paperwork, scholarship applications, and so much more that seniors do. It was exhausting. I finally had to realize I was not too old to pull all-nighters to get done what was needed. I often called myself the Deadline Momma because there was so much to handle. Frustration and anger sprouted. After all, Bruce's deceit had changed our lives forever.

Second Wife Janene

At this point, I'd had enough and decided to go on the offensive. Instead of taking the arrows, I boldly contacted Bruce's second wife, Janene, and asked if we could meet. She agreed but stated she would have to make it short.

My voice was suddenly shaking. "Thank you for your time. May I be rather blunt and ask why you and Bruce divorced?"

Janene was quick to respond. "He was a sociopath and took me for all my money. I wish I was financially capable of taking him to court, because he deserves justice. He put me through a hell I can't describe. It takes a person living it to know it."

My heart broke for her. I knew full well what it felt like to be ruined by a con man. "My daughter and I are living it now. I'm so sorry you had to go through that."

Janene shook her head, pain showing in her eyes. "Did he tell anyone you had leukemia, Becca?"

Shocked, I barked out, "What? I don't think so, why?"

"He lied to his boss and told him that I had leukemia. He hadn't been going to see his clients and lied, saying he'd missed the appointments because he had to take me to my doctor's appointments. That was the furthest from the truth. I *never* had leukemia. I thought he was working as usual. We both left the house for work at the same time every day, or so I thought. I assumed he was going to work. I don't know to this day where he went or what he really did all those days, but it wasn't helping me with leukemia. Whatever he did, I am sure it was deplorable!"

The more I listened to her cold, educated, and bitter voice, the more I realized I was just one of the many people Bruce used for his benefit—one more victim in his path. It was his pattern, his deranged way of life.

Letters from Janene

One day I was surprised to receive an email from Janene. It read:

Becca, I know it must have taken a lot of nerve to contact me earlier. I appreciate your persistence and desire to get your many questions answered. We have a lot in common as Bruce's victims. We both have been a part of his evil world. We both are just one of his many victims.

She'd also forwarded two emails Bruce had recently sent her. In them, he shared how sorry he was for the hurt he'd put her through. He also wanted to tell her how beautiful she was in the pictures he'd found online. The email address he'd used was one I'd never seen before. When did this man sleep? Every time I heard from someone, he was up to something evil and corrupt.

Chapter 40

SECRET DUPLEX SURPRISES

GAMES AND DECEIT

When I learned that my credit card statements were being mailed to Bruce's duplex's address, I called the manager. Bruce had convinced her he was a man of goodness and compassion. She almost cried when I told her what he had done to us and how Lauren had grown to love Bruce over the time he had lived there.

She shared his backstory with me, likely to check out its truthfulness. "Bruce told me about his great-niece. Is what he said true? I am suspicious now."

I was confused. He'd not mentioned any great-niece to me. "What about her?" I asked, not wanting to say for sure. Maybe I'd forgotten?

"He was traveling to see her in California a lot. It was why he was late paying rent. He said her parents died in a car accident and his niece didn't have her parents to take care of her anymore." She paused, as if waiting for me to respond.

I was too shocked to reply. None of this was true.

"He said he spent all of his time and money to help her?" The last word was lifted in a question. She waited for my response.

Shocked, I paused, then as kindly as I could tell her, I stammered, "This story is just another of Bruce's lies! I've never heard of a niece in California."

The manager paused for a long time, then finally said in a hoarse voice, "You're kidding me. I'm just heartbroken that Bruce lied to me. I considered him a friend. Ma'am, I listened to his lies over and over and let him convince me to accept his late payments."

"I'm so sorry to tell you," I sniffed. "You're just another one of his victims. Every week I find out about some other scheme he was involved in." He was grooming her, just as he had me. I quickly confirmed with Bruce's brother there was no great-niece in California.

Soon after, Bruce was evicted from the duplex. When Bruce moved out, he took everything. I knew some of my belongings were there, items we once had in storage. I saw them on Thanksgiving, the day Lauren and I surprised him. Where was the rest of my stuff he'd stolen? Where were the numerous totes he used to hide my business files? I've never recovered any of my things.

According to my divorce attorney, it was my word against his. I had no proof that those items ever existed, especially since I couldn't list them individually. It never occurred to me to take pictures of my things. He told me to look at the big picture and realize it wasn't worth battling over in court unless I could prove he had them.

He stole precious family heirlooms, yet he couldn't care less about them. The irony—I had taken such care of his family's things with his brothers to make sure they were safely stored until the courts decided who got what.

Hot Check

The duplex manager called me a few weeks after he moved out. I was shocked to hear from her again. She told me, "Bruce was evicted because of a hot check for $5,500. Do you realize I almost got fired because I believed every lie Bruce told me about why he wasn't able to pay the rent? Bruce Walker is the best con artist I've ever known." The tone in her voice made me wonder if he was more involved with her than it seemed.

I should have expected more deceit from the man I used to love, but at this point, after everything Bruce had pulled, I could only shake my head. "I'm so sorry. I didn't even know he was still renting that place until I called you a few weeks ago."

She paused on the line, as if she were about to say something uncomfortable. "Becca, I'm sorry to say this to you. But we've had to put a $5,500 lien on your house to cover the hot check. I hope this doesn't put you in a bad spot, but we have to get the money, and that is what the management company decided to do."

My blood boiled. "No, do you have to do that? Isn't there another way?"

"I'm afraid there isn't. He wrote hot checks, he lied..." She trailed off then added, "I'm just glad he removed all the guns he had in there. Now I'm wondering what else he was up to. Were they even registered?"

"Guns?" My heart skipped a beat. "I have no idea about any guns other than his father's two antique guns he showed me when we were dating."

"I need to go. Someone is here. Becca, I'm sorry to be the bearer of bad news."

My hands were shaking uncontrollably as I said my goodbye and hung up. When I calmed down, I called my attorney, who confirmed they had a right to collect what Bruce owed, and since we both owned the house, it was legal. I wondered what other repercussions I'd have to suffer because of his criminal behavior.

I stayed up all night thinking of the duplex. Why did he keep it all that time? I couldn't help but think about his pornography and bestiality habits, copies of the many receipts from my credit cards, extra clothes, groceries, girlfriends, etc. Why did he have so many guns and where did they end up? Detective Sheets verified that there were no records from pawn shops that they were sold. I prayed for strength to get through the divorce, where hopefully the surprises would end, the games would be played out, and he would be out of my life forever. I also prayed he no longer had the weapons.

Ivy Avenue Landlord

The phone rang and rang one morning. My sluggish body dragged out of bed and answered the call. An irate woman barked at me, "I don't mean to be rude, but can you tell me when Bruce is going to pay your last month's rent?" It was our previous landlord, the lady who owned the house we rented on Ivy Avenue while building our new house.

Was I hearing her correctly? For the next twenty minutes I listened to her complain about Bruce's irresponsible nature.

Her shrill voice rang in my ear. "Bruce had been late on most every month's rent, and I was not renewing your lease or allowing you to rent month-to-month. You were basically evicted!" This was news to me, but it explained why we were forced to move into our newly built home, even with much of it still left to finish.

I apologized profusely and didn't even have the energy to explain what I'd been going through. My mind and body became numb as I heard very few words. It was like being in a never-ending boxing match. Every day his devious lies came back to punch me in the gut and take away another part of my life. No matter how much I healed in between these bouts, it brought me to rock bottom again having to listen to the lies he'd tossed around like candy at the Christmas parade. Every part of our shared life was full of his deceit.

House on the Market

I felt sure that the house we had built and lived in from May through October would sell quickly, since it was such a beautiful home. Bruce had added many special features, including built-ins in every room, large storage closets, a unique pool house, spacious windows, a large basement, a beautiful pool and waterfall, wide hallways, stone accent walls, a safe room, and numerous other amenities. It had been my dream home.

Jace Kirkpatrick's name showed up on my phone as it was ringing one Friday night as I was dozing off watching mindless TV.

I couldn't imagine the successful realtor taking time to call me, especially at the end of the business week.

"Becca, I hate to bother you, but I need to bring something to your attention. After several months of dealing with Bruce, we must remove him from the selling process. Every time we have a buyer, Bruce disagrees with the offered price."

"This is another one of his games. He doesn't listen to a thing I say. In fact, we normally go through my attorney to communicate."

"Great idea! I would encourage you to get your attorney to convince Bruce it is in the best interest of both of you to remove him from selling the house. I think I can sell it quickly if he isn't involved."

My divorce attorney called a few weeks later to tell me Bruce was finally willing to sign an agreement to exclude himself from the sale of the home. Although I paid for several of their phone conversations, I was relieved Bruce had agreed. Maybe I wouldn't have to foreclose after all.

Six weeks later, at the end of a long workday, I walked in the door, took off my shoes, and fell onto my bed. I'd looked forward to wrapping up tight in a soft blanket and taking a good long nap all week long. The phone rang but I was tempted to let it go to voicemail. When I saw Jace Kirkpatrick's office number, I grabbed the phone with excitement and hope. Had they found a potential buyer?

Jace's office manager was on the line. Her voice said it all. More bad news. Bruce had swindled us all once again. When he was in the realtor's office to sign the agreement that released him from being involved in selling the home, he secretly wrote a note stating that he was to be notified and included in all offers of the sale of the home. Evidently, Bruce had written this when the manager stepped out of the conference room for just a few minutes. He was evil.

Everything I was trying to do to help the dream house sell back-fired. Bruce was doing whatever he could think of to put obstacles in my way. It was ALL a game to him.

There was nothing Jace or the office manager could do other than apologize over and over to me. With a growing lack of trust in people, we foreclosed on the house. My dreams of the perfect house went up in flames. Bruce knew how to cheat and win. After all, he was an expert. I'm sure he rejoiced the day we foreclosed. Another checkmate. Another burning of my dreams.

Chapter 41

COPING THROUGH FAITH

AT THAT TIME IN my life, I claimed a certain Bible verse as my own, a verse I would live by:

"Peace I leave with you; My peace I give you. I do not give to you as the world gives. Do not let your hearts be troubled and do not be afraid" (John 14:27 NIV).

I would repeat it over and over as I drove, dressed for work, went to the courtroom, met with my divorce attorney, or tried to go to sleep at night. I truly could always feel Jesus' peace and under ALL circumstances if I would just intentionally focus on Jesus. I did not have to wait for my world to quit spinning, or for a new day to occur without problems, but thankfully, I could feel HIS peace in the storm. I know it seems impossible to think I could feel peace in the midst of such turmoil in my life, but I discovered Jesus is the answer. Having a relationship with Jesus is like no other relationship.

I tried to explain to a friend how I was forced to take one day at a time, and sometimes one hour at a time. It surprised me, but I did worry less than I had in the past. She did not understand until I explained it this way. If I looked too far in the future, anxiety would rob me of any joy God wanted me to have that day. My world would start spinning uncontrollably. To keep from becoming overwhelmed, I tried to focus on the present moment. The more I read scriptures, the more at peace I felt.

Notebook

Keeping my life organized also helped me cope. I wrote notes throughout the day and night, trying to keep a diary of dates, responsibilities, phone calls, and prayers. I had a notebook tabbed for Bible verses, bankers, attorneys, realtors, detectives, and FBI a gents.

When I look back at the monumental amount of paperwork and contacts I needed to deal with on a consistent basis, I know Jesus was with me every step of the way. I had two banks to deal with often and another I dealt with for Bruce's secret safety deposit box. I had the builder, the pool man, the fence company, the security department at work, two attorneys, a realtor, an identity theft officer, the FBI, the IRS, and my detective. Thankfully, I knew with Jesus I would see the light as He held my hand through it all.

Lunch with Mom

One day Mom and I were eating lunch together when she told me she greatly admired my smile and positive attitude, especially at such a difficult time in my life.

She asked, "How do you do it?"

I asked her what she meant.

Mom blinked away tears. "You are strong, hopeful, and positive, yet you have gone through a great tragedy. How do you have that great attitude?"

I told her it had to be Jesus because it sure was not me. Truthfully, it was Jesus! I got up from the table and gave my heartbroken mother a hug. My arms held her tight. I didn't want to let go.

I gathered my emotions and shared, "Mom, this is how Jesus is. He wants to put His loving arms around you and let you know Lauren and I will be okay. You will be okay. We just have to trust Him."

My Faith

I leaned on my faith every single day. I kept reminding myself that what I was experiencing was just a small segment of my life and I was not yet even fifty years old. Bruce had robbed me of all the joy he was ever going to because Jesus was with me every step of the way! He had masqueraded as a savior to me, but Jesus is my only Savior.

To put everything in a better perspective, I visualized a timeline starting at age one and going into the 80s and 90s—my life's expectancy. I carried an index card with me. I drew a timeline on one side, which was a visual tool of all the life I had left to live. What I was experiencing with Bruce was a moment in time. The best part was at the end of the timeline I would be in Heaven, knowing that Jesus was my Lord and Savior. On the other side of the index card, I wrote: "Peace I leave with you. My peace I give to you. I do not give to you as the world gives. Do not let your heart be troubled and do not be afraid" (John 14:27).

The visual reminders helped me to feel Jesus' love and comfort. Jesus has given me unexpected opportunities to share the index card with others over the years. I always pray that it gives others strength too.

Chapter 42

LETTERS FROM BRUCE

APRIL 2007

I ran to my mailbox one rainy day and opened an envelope with no return address. It was a letter from Bruce. My life was busy enough without another one of Bruce's demented games. The letter read:

Dearest Becca,

You may want to tell yourself that you don't know me, or you never really did, but I find this a sad choice. You know better. So do I. I am sincerely the same person you befriended, you fell for, and I fell for you unexpectedly. I am the man that would still to this day do anything for you and Lauren.

We could have taken different paths than we did when I hurt you so terribly. The one you chose has left us unable to communicate, heal, or even help one another, even in the smallest of ways. It is sad to go from incredible love at a million miles an hour to where we are now. I know I have hurt you and Lauren, and that knowledge is difficult for me. You are the two I never meant to cause pain. This is sad to me. I believe you do love me even now, but we are still here not communicating at all. That is sad.

We spent so much time together and we both felt we didn't want to be anywhere else. You and I were so willing to forgo "ourselves" for each other's benefits. We cared so deeply about each other, and our lives are so different apart. We will always feel there is something missing in ourselves without that connection. I miss our willingness to do whatever it took to make each other content and safeguard them from harm. Unconditional love like that should continue through the good times and bad and could lift our spirits higher than we could ever imagine or drop into the depths of despair. In my eyes, that is love, but Corinthians says it better than I can. "Love is patient and kind; love is not jealous or boastful; it is not arrogant or rude. Love does not insist on its own way; it is not irritable or resentful; it does not rejoice at wrong but rejoices in the light. Love bears all things; believes all things; hopes all things; endures all things."

I plan on facing the charges against me. Then try to find a living that can meet my debts and then gives me a way to contribute to a better life for you. I don't know how this will work out, but we'll find out. I'm staying here and have no plans to move away from the area unless the courts require it.

Bruce

I did not answer him. I mourned the loss of a man I once believed in wholeheartedly. I fully expected him to reach out to me at some point, but this letter was difficult to read. Did he really think love could conquer so many deceptions, so many criminal acts, and his utter disrespect for the false devotion to God? For Bruce to speak of this unconditional love was just another game. Likely he was in between victims and was reminiscing of what we once had.

I knew all of this was a lie. He'd shown me in a hundred ways there was no room for love between us. The man I thought of as THE Jackson Bruce Walker had destroyed any chance at that in the short time we were married.

May 2007

A month later, Bruce sent me an email with his best advice for me, packed in a selfish, deceitful few words. My hands shook as I scrolled down to read what he sent me.

```
I wanted to write to you before the house
is sold. There is another option you should
consider—bankruptcy. If you choose this
path, I can transfer the deed to your name
after you've declared bankruptcy, and it
is finalized. This will allow you the sale
of the house at a profit, then you can
put this toward Lauren's college expenses.
The matters of the heart are even more
difficult than these decisions.
```

```
Praying you and Lauren are doing well,
Bruce
```

Clicking off the computer screen did not help my shaking. This was only one more attempt to play his sick-minded games. I was simply a pawn that he toyed with. It was as if we were playing Monopoly with play money as far as Bruce was concerned.

How dare he! His words, "you should consider—bankruptcy," lit my fuse. Who was he to be giving me "advice" to consider? All the advice he gave was either to play a mind game with me or for him to benefit in some way. He was relentless. After all the deceit, did he really think I would trust him to transfer the deed and put it in my name? What a joke.

The likelihood of me being forced to file for bankruptcy in the future, after our divorce would be finalized, was hard enough to stomach. Unfortunately, he was winning this game, and I could do nothing about it.

Chapter 43

GRADUATION DAY

LAUREN'S GRADUATION

April and May were extra-busy months. Lauren was running from here to there with senior year activities, working two jobs, and completing schoolwork. I was working, meeting with attorneys, and trying to find special time with Lauren. We both tried to talk about fun things, ordinary things, anything other than Bruce. He had robbed us both of too much time already. I was extremely proud of Lauren for being strong, and able to juggle the turmoil, uncertainties, and loss during her senior year.

On graduation day, I woke, and anxiety hit me hard the moment my eyes opened. I desperately wanted this day to be perfect for Lauren. She deserved the happiest graduation day there ever was. Her dad, Scott, and his family were coming from out of town. My family was coming as well. We all wanted to sit together, so I knew I had to get to the arena early to save a large number of seats. I worried I wouldn't find the perfect seats for all of us to see Lauren easily. I wanted her to know where we were. Details were rattling in my head.

Passing by a mirror, I saw my face. Bags under my eyes made me look like I hadn't slept in days. The year had certainly aged me. I brushed it off. Today was about Lauren and we had much to celebrate!

The day was full of bittersweet emotion. Mom and I sat next to each other and held hands off and on during the ceremony. When I watched my daughter walk across the stage to get her diploma,

I used one tissue after another, wiping away happy and sad tears. As she looked up in the stands and our eyes locked, I knew we were thinking of the same thing. We survived the year. We loved each other, and we were strong. Later I saw Lauren and her friends laugh, joke, and smile from ear to ear. Seeing Lauren happy was priceless. I was grateful I could put all my energy into focusing on the positive things the day had to offer. It was a conscious choice to see the time we lost as a glass half-full and be thankful my daughter and I were alive and well. A glass full of promise for our future.

The scriptures tell us: "He gives power to the weak and strength to the powerless" (Isaiah 40:29 NLT).

What renewed hope and strength I felt knowing the truth in the scripture. My cup runneth over. Healing was beginning.

New Homeowners

After the glow of graduation, life settled back to semi-normal. I'd had a counseling session, and I felt emotionally strong and at peace. I glanced back at blueprints, unused hardware, and other items in the back seat of my car that we'd not had a chance to use in the new dream house. I knew a prominent family had purchased it, which made me happy knowing it wasn't sitting empty any longer.

Without hesitation, I drove to the house, thinking about the Bible Bruce and I set under the foundation and then had to foreclose on soon after. I planned to leave these items on the porch, but when I saw the curtain open and the lights on, I spontaneously walked to the front door and rang the doorbell. I was trying to stay strong.

A lady answered the door with a shy smile, and in the background, I saw a little girl playing. "Yes, may I help you?"

I tried not to focus on how different everything looked with the changes they'd made, with their furniture instead of ours. I couldn't help but notice they had almost the same round table and chairs in the dining room as we had. I refocused and held out the rolled-up blueprint and bag of hardware. "I'm the previous owner and I felt you should have these."

She stepped out onto the stoop and took them from me. "How sweet of you to bring them over. Thank you."

I smiled and held back all the pain this house had dealt me. "No worries. Have a great day."

I didn't want to squelch the joy she felt about her new home by being tearful or sad. Simply, I was excited for them to have this beautiful home to live in and make better memories.

I walked away saying, "God bless you!"

Jesus was helping me every step I took as I walked to my car. I kept telling Him that I couldn't do this alone. That had been my dream home, yet seeing a little girl there, now her home, made everything real. It was never going to be Lauren's home, although we made several happy memories there. It was never going to be my home. We were never going to have pool parties or church group gatherings there. Those dreams never came to fruition.

I drove to the next block and stopped the car. Looking up in the sky, I asked God to help me look to the future, to help me close this chapter in my life. As I watched, the sun brightened. It must have come out from behind a cloud. I saw it as God telling me I had brighter days ahead. He was asking me to just trust Him.

PART 4 TRIALS AND COURT DATES

Chapter 44

THE DIVORCE HEARINGS

NOTEBOOK

The notebook I kept with sections for each compartment of my life seemed to expand rapidly as I gathered information for the divorce hearings and other areas of my new life. Each of the five hearings required a great amount of homework on my part. Black circles were under my eyes most days; sleep was not a priority. I had to work, then take care of responsibilities. I certainly wanted to be the mom that Lauren deserved and give her what she needed in this time of turmoil.

In typical Bruce fashion, he loved to play mind games and make me spend money on senseless things. He used the court cases for his amusement. Since he was representing himself, he took full advantage of the situation by calling my attorney incessantly. When Bruce contacted him, he would do his best to limit the conversations but warned me I would still be responsible for the time billed, just as if Bruce were another attorney. These games racked up my bills, but the real damage was the constant emotional toll. Even though I had no real contact with Bruce, he was still hitting me where it hurt—my pocketbook. Just another way I had no control over my life.

Preparing for the Divorce Hearings

We spent endless hours preparing for the court dates. Surprisingly, I got my work done in my office at the hospital, but my phone was ringing off the wall most days with either Dillon, Detective Sheets, or Mr. Phillips. A lot of it was for the house, my income from Bruce, and who was to pay what.

To prepare for the court dates that were spaced across the calendar for months, there were seemingly endless depositions, strategy meetings, interviews, paperwork, inventories, and divorce proceedings. There were too many to recall, too painful to relive. Some I wish I could forget.

There were so many people who were connected and affected by the building and selling of the house alone—the builder, fencing guy, landscaper, real estate agent, and who knows who else. My lawyers handled most of the complicated elements, and I showed up and told my side whenever they needed it.

We had to come to an agreement about what to do with all our shared assets and how to divide them fairly. I spent hours and hours taking pictures and documenting everything in the dream house, who came into the marriage with what, and capturing what was in various storage units that I knew about, including the one Mike and Doug were paying for that held their family heirlooms. It was overwhelming trying to keep track of everything by taking pictures and logging each item by number. Eventually the courts awarded most of those items to me, and then Bruce's brothers and I negotiated a fair price for what they wanted to keep.

Time in Court

Time stood still. I clenched my teeth as I sat on the front bench of the large courtroom between Mr. Phillips and my mother. The lights were bright; the mahogany walls and pews were dark and shiny. My side of the large courtroom was full of friends and loved ones who wanted to show their support. Bruce was alone and sitting on the other side in the front row by himself. The tension was as thick as thistles.

This was the third hearing we had on the calendar, so at least I had gotten some practice and was somewhat aware of the games Bruce played. Mr. Phillips had briefed me before we walked into the courtroom, but suddenly I had a million questions. I shook as my mom placed her hand on my leg, patting and whispering, "It will be okay. Don't you worry because it will be okay," just as she had reminded me when we were driving away from our burning house almost forty years ago.

While we were waiting for the judge to appear, Bruce stood up and changed seats, crossing to the other side of the aisle directly behind Lauren in the third row! I knew he was trying to get a reaction out of me, but I kept my cool and said nothing.

Lauren had experienced every emotion from extreme sadness to great anguish through this nightmare since the evening I told her Bruce was a fraud. Today in the courtroom she was angry, not for herself, but for me. She was furious Bruce was playing more games, trying to hurt us. She knew he was a sick man without a heart. I watched her carefully, willing her not to react as her eyes met the bailiffs'.

I prayed, "Sweet Jesus, send her strength to keep her cool."

Lauren was sitting with Stefanie, her closest friend, and Brenda, her mom, and they grabbed her hands for support. I was so proud of her at that moment. It took a lot to keep from lashing out at the betrayal, the lies, the games. But my daughter had grown stronger through this horrific experience. I blinked away tears of pride. I knew, despite the damage he'd caused, Lauren would get through this stronger and better equipped in life than I had been.

It seemed like hours before the judge entered the room, but when he did, we all stood, and I immediately felt lightheaded. Was I about to faint? Surely not. I didn't want to give that evil Jackson Bruce Walker the satisfaction of me not able to handle the stress he put me through.

It was difficult enough to sit in the same courtroom with him, but to make matters worse, he was allowed to ask me direct questions while I was on the stand since he was representing himself. He used the time to make me squirm, crafting condescending questions, needling me every chance he could. It was a game to him, and he loved to play it. He repeated questions, asking me specific dollar amounts, knowing I was nervous and wouldn't remember. His intentions were cruel, as if the entire point was to hurt me, not prove his innocence.

I still remember his devious smile as he asked, "Surely, Becca, you remember the amount of your car payment, don't you?"

"Well, I'm not exactly sure of the amount this morning, something around $350."

When I answered, his smile turned into a smirk and he asked, "Now surely you have a better memory than that. Let me ask you the same question but in another way. That may help you."

I felt every eye in the room looking at me while on the stand. It was as if time stood still. I wanted them to see through his lies and condescending questions. He was good at manipulating people into liking him. *Please, judge, don't be fooled by this heinous man.*

The words he spoke did not affect me as much as the tone in his voice and look on his face. I wanted to scream at him, yet that was exactly what he wanted me to do. I felt enormous pressure on the stand, and he used this to try to force me to look unstable, to lose my temper and look crazy. I resisted, somehow. I felt Jesus' presence with me then.

My legs were weak as I held onto the mahogany banister that led me to my seat. I knew not to look at Mom or Lauren, or anyone for that matter. I had to keep my composure. It was now Bruce's turn to answer questions.

My attorney stood and approached the bench. "Where are you living these days, Mr. Walker?"

Bruce kept a straight face and looked as pitiful as possible, looking for sympathy. "Mainly in my car."

Mr. Phillips presented several checks Bruce had written from his new checking account: Steak Express for forty-two dollars and Pizza Hut for forty-five dollars. The questions were met with silence.

"It seems rather odd to me that if you are living in your car, why did you spend so much on these meals? You had no way of refrigerating leftovers. Were you possibly buying meals for other people?"

Whatever his answers were, they were all lies. Bruce didn't know how to tell the truth. It was obvious to me he was buying dinner to groom someone to be his next victim. Wouldn't the judge see through Bruce's complete inability to tell the truth?

The judge spoke a few words before we were adjourned, awarding me some of Bruce's possessions. Fury was bubbling up inside of me and I swallowed it down with disgust. All I could focus on was how the man before me was a liar, a cheat, and a thief.

After the hearing, I walked into the refreshment room next door for a bottle of water. Bruce followed behind me, wanting to do or say anything to get me to make a scene. My skin was crawling just being that close to him.

I turned on him and said, "I don't know how you can live with yourself." How I wanted to yell, scream, and kick, but I kept my cool. There were so many things I wanted to say, but I knew this was not the place or time.

Bruce smiled sweetly. "It was SO good to see your mother today. She looks amazing!"

Every word was calculated to get a reaction out of me. It was all I could do to keep my composure. It took everything in me to not slap his face with all my might. It was all a game to him. He had no feelings, no compassion, no sorrow, and no heart. He was only a shell of a person with a sick mind.

I felt nauseous and left the room, took the elevator down to the lobby, and made it outside before I threw up on the courthouse lawn. How could he be the same man I remember helping me find answers to my medical issues, who laughed lovingly with me as I suffered through my stomach issues?

Diamond Ring, Guns, and Coin Collection

In the next few days, Detective Sheets called me with a puzzling find. "Becca, I have a question for you. I know you are at work so I will make this quick. Did you have a six-diamond wedding ring or dinner ring by any chance?"

Instinctively, I glanced at my left ring finger. "No, I don't. Why?"

"Bruce sold a ring with six diamonds to a pawn shop in December here in the area. I was wondering if it was yours."

We hung up and it left me wondering. I'd never seen a ring with six diamonds the entire time we were together. Was this a ring he was going to give his first wife when he was engaged to both of us? Or was this his mother's ring his brothers knew nothing about? Or another possibility. Had Bruce stolen it? Questions continued to pop up.

Next time I spoke with Mr. Phillips, I mentioned it. He made sure to ask Bruce about it in the next hearing a few weeks away.

During the hearing, he asked, "There is a record of you selling a diamond ring to a nearby pawn shop. Do you recall whose it was?"

Bruce glanced at me, then down at his hands, and I had the distinct impression he was making up an answer on the fly. "Yes, it was a family heirloom. I hated to sell it, but I needed the money."

Mr. Philips continued. "And you had a number of guns in your possession when you and Becca were living under one roof. Is that correct?"

"Yes, they were my dad's, but I have sold them all, again because I needed the money."

A stab of fear tore through my heart. The thought of this unstable man owning guns in the house we shared... I glanced back at Lauren, whose eyes were wide. It could have been so much worse. I thanked God for keeping us safe during those months we were with him, and after as he stalked us.

"You received $20,000 recently from selling a coin collection. Where is that money?" Mr. Phillips paced as he waited for another lie.

Bruce's words spewed from his mouth like venom. We never learned the truth.

Once I'd cut off my income from his greedy hands, he had to get money from somewhere. I knew he was lying on the stand, but there was no way to prove where the ring, guns, and coins had come from or what he had really done with them.

Chapter 45

REPERCUSSIONS

STORAGE UNIT

During one of the hearings, I was awarded the computers and electronic items in a storage unit Bruce had rented for the past two years without my knowledge. While I was relieved to have some benefit from Bruce's lies, I was afraid to collect the items. I knew he would probably show up when I came to empty it.

Because of my work schedule, I needed to wait until the last day of the month to go to the storage unit. If I did not get it emptied that day, the items would be the property of the storage company because Bruce had quit paying the monthly fee several months prior. I asked friends if they could meet me there as protection and to try to make the process faster. I was grateful for their support.

I was shaking almost the entire time we were there. As we began moving the boxes, my phone rang. It was one of my close friends heading to the unit to help. "Becca, I'm sorry I am running late. I made a wrong turn and was at the back of the storage property where I saw Bruce's SUV hidden. He's in it. I know he saw me."

Bruce must have gotten there before the sun came up because I was there at the crack of dawn. We would have seen him entering if he'd arrived after us. Minutes later, Bruce showed up laughing and shaking his head. I remember the sound of every step he took while shuffling slowly down the dark hallway between the units, one foot in front of the other. He had no remorse as he stared me down with dull, shallow eyes. His hands were in his pockets as if he was hiding something. Every nerve in my body was firing! It took tremendous self-control to not hit him with all my might. I'm confident Jesus took control of the situation, though, not me.

I had no idea if he had a gun with him, but it was obvious his intention was to scare me just as he intended to Thanksgiving Day. My friends ignored him and continued to move boxes. He may have only been there for two or three minutes, but to me it seemed like an eternity. I wonder if he'd hope to scare us off and take the rest of the boxes with him. Either way, it was unnerving. I was furious he'd made me react again. All of this was just another way to intimidate me, another cat-and-mouse game.

Who was this man? It was as though he was a stranger who knew nothing but evil, not the person who'd fooled me for nearly eighteen months. The real Bruce was showing through the facade he'd shown me for several years.

Garage Sale

I was clueless as to what most of the equipment was, much less what it was worth. I asked a friend to help me do some research so we could get a fair value for them in a garage sale. A lot of it was too old or out of date to be worth much. I wondered who would buy any of it, and for that matter why did Bruce have it in the first place? Why was he spending money on a storage unit to store old computer parts? The sale put a little over $300 in my pocket, which was a great disappointment, but at least it was something to help pay a few bills.

Chapter 46

THE ORANGE JUMPSUIT

AUGUST 2007

I have been embarrassed before, but nothing like when I turned on the television to see the news reporting Jackson Bruce Walker was missing. He'd been set to appear in federal court for the false collateral he presented to the mortgage company, but no one could find him. My first thought was to lock the doors. He was becoming more unstable, and I worried he'd be paying me a visit.

Later that day at work, I found a newspaper article with Bruce's mug shot with his bond set for $10,000 and another claiming he was missing and wanted by the police.

Scared and furious, I sat down at my computer and typed out an email to Bruce. "Be a man and turn yourself in. This is so embarrassing. You are in the paper and on all the news channels. Be a man and do the right thing!"

I called Detective Sheets, and she advised me to post his picture in a visible area in the break room with a notice to call 911 right away if anyone saw him. His behavior had been so erratic and unlike the man I once knew. It made me anxious and nervous, always looking over my shoulder. I was afraid he would show up and make a scene.

We were the talk of the town once again. I tried to hold my head up high like my daddy would have told me, if he had been alive, but some days were harder than others. My coworkers were so supportive, promising they'd keep an eye out for him, checking on me throughout the day, walking me to my car at the end of the day. I was immensely grateful.

A few days later, on a busy weekday morning, I was walking into my office at the hospital when my cell phone rang. It was Bruce's friend, Brian, who was almost out of breath. "I just watched Bruce get picked up by the police at McDonald's near Bellar Avenue. His car is being impounded!"

I was washed in relief. "You're kidding?" Finally, I could watch the news without seeing his face. I let out a sigh of relief. "Thank you, Brian. Let me know if you hear anything else."

I called Lauren immediately and we both cried over the phone. We could finally take a deep breath and sleep soundly that night. The constant worry about what new bomb he would drop on us was over. He was apprehended and hopefully would be locked up and out of our lives.

Bruce's Verdict and Sentencing

Months later I was enjoying watching autumn leaves fall from the trees outside my office window when the phone rang. "Becca, this is Detective Sheets. I have some good news. Bruce's federal criminal trial is ending. I wondered if you wanted to be in the courtroom."

My heart sped up. This meant the ordeal was over. If he was sent to jail, he wouldn't be around to stalk me or play any more games. "Yes, I think I need to see this with my own two eyes. It still just doesn't seem real to me." I jotted down the date and time and readied myself to face him again.

The last day of the trial, I left work just in time to be there. I stood next to my car, watching a small group of prisoners walk across the street. To my horror, I saw Bruce in the pack. It was unimaginable. My head felt light, as though I was about to faint. My heart stopped. I was totally unprepared.

Seeing him made it real. I never dreamed I would be married to a man who wore an orange jumpsuit and handcuffs. It was hard enough to see his mug shot on the news, but this was more than I imagined. How could that prisoner be the man I had married and was now divorcing? Where did my Bruce go? Where was the man who had been such a loving caretaker to his mom and me?

It was hard for my mind to fathom what had happened to us over the last eighteen months. I knew it was crucial to be present at the time of sentencing, to see with my own two eyes, to witness justice prevail.

In the courtroom, our eyes met. Bruce's were filled with rage. I'd never seen that anger in him through all the terrible things he'd done to us. I could read his expression though. He blamed me for his circumstances. It was as if he'd done nothing wrong. There was no shame or remorse. He felt no guilt. Only fury that he'd been caught.

I felt numb. I don't remember anyone explaining to me how long the trial had been or how long the deliberation would be. I was merely existing as I watched the man in the orange jumpsuit. I have no idea who read the verdict, but it was a surreal moment. It was as though I was living someone else's life. I was relieved and yet felt empty inside. The man who once gave me medicine morning and night in a caring manner was now looking at me with evil and angry eyes. I came alone to the courthouse and yet I didn't feel alone. When I thought I couldn't watch Bruce Walker in the orange jumpsuit with handcuffs on anymore, I shut my eyes and prayed. I instantly felt Jesus' presence. He never left me.

Sitting in the back row of the courtroom, I watched Bruce stand with handcuffs around his wrists, listening to someone state his verdict: "Jackson Bruce Walker, guilty, to one count of making a false statement to a bank."

I was stuck on the verdict. I was relieved he was guilty, but after all the things he'd done to us, to the bank, he was convicted of a false statement? The man had stolen my life savings, defrauded the bank, kited checks. It was so much more than a false statement to a bank. I sat there with my mind spinning, trying to make sense of this. He deserved to be behind bars for a long time. After all, this was not his first offense. He'd been in jail before for writing hot checks.

In the end Jackson Bruce Walker was sentenced to a "white-collar prison" for only sixteen months, followed by four years of supervised release. He was ordered to pay the bank back close to $65,000. The minor consequences for such a liar sickened me. The bank would get their money eventually, but what about me? What about Lauren? Where was our retribution? How were we going to be made whole after all he'd put us through? After all he'd stolen from us? I was devastated. I had, unrealistically, thought he'd be in prison for years and years, giving us a hiatus from his psychological abuse, his criminal activities...the stalking.

After Prison

Bruce served his time, and soon after he was released, he returned to our community. Sixteen months passed in a flash, and I was again looking over my shoulder, waiting for the other shoe to drop, terrified he'd show up around the corner with that evil smirk.

Unfortunately, Lauren ran into him before I did. She frantically called me from the McDonald's bathroom. The same one where he'd been apprehended. "Mom, you're not going to believe who I saw today!" It was difficult to hear what she was saying through the tears and anguish. "Bruce was at McDonald's with another lady and a little boy. We saw each other. Mom, I thought I would never have to see him again. What were the chances of us going to the same place to eat after all this time?"

He was in the drive-through in a silver SUV with a lady in the front seat and a young boy in the back seat. Lauren was inside ordering her meal when their eyes met. Both took a double take before Lauren sprinted to the restroom to call me, ready to kick and spit nails.

"Lauren, stay put. Wait awhile before you leave." I stayed on the phone with her while she calmed down and we waited for him to leave.

"Mom." Her voice was calmer now. "I just have this terrible feeling he's in that SUV with another victim and her innocent little boy in the back seat."

My face flushed with a mixture of anger, fear, and nausea. She was right. He was back to what he'd been so good at. It broke my heart knowing this little boy's world would crumble one day, just as mine and Lauren's had.

Chapter 47

HOW THIS CHANGED ME

THE LAST TIME I saw Bruce, he was wearing the orange jumpsuit and handcuffs in the courtroom. When I looked into his eyes, they were empty blue shells completely void of sorrow or regret. Where did he go? Where was the man I was going to grow old with and raise grandchildren with? Where was the man who was nurturing, caring, who was my best friend, my husband? I had loved that man, although I did not know him at all, but only the person he pretended to be. It was as if he'd died.

It was all a lie. Our marriage was a lie. I can't help but wonder if he ever really loved me or was it just a means to steal my hard-earned money and abuse my good credit. He'd taken advantage of me because of my poor health. My vulnerability as a single mother. Sadly, I knew the answer.

I mourned the loss of the young, innocent me. Where was the little girl who'd trusted others, who'd talked to strangers, felt secure, and who easily shared openly with others? What had happened to that high school girl selected as most likely to succeed? I'd always thought of myself as a leader rather than a follower. I was no longer the naive, trusting person I'd always been. I now lived next to people I barely knew because I didn't feel safe enough to tell them my name. Sometimes I'd give out my UPS mailing address rather than my physical address because I did not want people to know where I lived. I'd become a shell of my former self, hiding away from fear of strangers. My view of myself and others around me changed completely. There were only a few people I trusted, and even then, I asked myself if I could really trust them at all.

How did I go so wrong? After all, I was a social worker and had studied personality disorders. I had read what a sociopath was. Why hadn't I recognized Bruce's classic behavior? Why had no one warned me about him, despite having multiple opportunities? I had more questions than I could count.

PTSD

Life throws us unexpected difficulties. I've certainly experienced them; we all have. After almost two years had passed, I felt as though my life was getting back on track. I was having a normal day, grocery shopping, and pulled out my credit card to pay, as I had hundreds of times before. This time my card was declined. I felt my face turn red, and I immediately felt perspiration above my upper lip.

The lady behind the counter patted my hand. "It's okay. This kind of thing happens all the time." She turned to the screen. "It's probably a glitch in the system. Do you have another card?"

She was oblivious to what I'd been through with Bruce. My hands were sweating, and my legs were weak. My physical response to this situation surprised me. My mind immediately took me back to the first time my credit card was declined, sweeping me to utter shock when I realized Bruce had maxed out all four of my credit cards. I was reliving the moment as deeply emotional as it had been two years ago. My fear was he'd done it again.

As a social worker I knew the meaning of PTSD, post-traumatic stress disorder. I'd helped several patients with it over the years. Instinctively I knew what my body was experiencing. My head knew the textbook definition, but all my body could feel was fear that made me want to run and keep on running.

I called my credit card company, and they explained someone had tried and failed to order something online, therefore they stopped all charges. It explained why my card was declined. Most people would be relieved, but I just kept wondering if Jackson Bruce Walker was playing games again.

Memories flooded back to the day years ago, when my accounts were frozen and I'd had a restraining order on Bruce yet he was still able to withdraw funds. PTSD had me sweating, fearing it would all start over again and I'd be right back in the bank office trying to figure out what happened to my life. I can't tell you how many times I relived those awful moments Bruce had put me through, but it was more than I'd ever expected.

Chapter 48

I WISH I HAD KNOWN

SOCIOPATH

The Mayo Clinic defines sociopathy: Antisocial personality disorder, sometimes called sociopathy, is a mental disorder in which a person consistently shows no regard for right and wrong and ignores the rights and feelings of others. People with antisocial personality disorder tend to antagonize, manipulate, or treat others harshly or with callous indifference. They show no guilt or remorse for their behavior. [1]

I wish I had known the man who made my heart skip a beat in the red sports car long ago was a crooked genius, able to smile, sway others emotionally, lie, and deceive in one breath. He was the charismatic con artist king.

I am not qualified to diagnose Bruce with antisocial personality disorder, or anything else for that matter. I simply wish I had known the truth of his past behavior when we were reacquainted in our forties. Sociopath tendencies were never on my radar.

I wish I'd done my homework before I ever let him into my life, even as a friend. I wish I had been more cautious and not so trusting. If I'd thought to order a background check at the very beginning, before we even thought of holding hands, Lauren and I would have been protected from so much heartache. It just wasn't

---

1. https://www.mayoclinic.org/diseases-conditions/antisocial
   -personality-disorder/symptoms-causes/syc-20353928

in my nature to be suspicious. I don't want to lose that side of me, the one who welcomes strangers with open arms. But I learned a hard lesson, one I wish I'd learned much earlier in life.

These sick-minded sociopaths, like Bruce, use others to get what they want. Rules and laws do not apply to them. Once they have drained their victim of everything they can, they move on to the next without hesitation.

Most share little truth about their past. Bruce was a listener, always wanting to ask questions to get to know other people, rather than sharing about himself. They are amazing manipulators who initially invest heavily in their victims. They pretend to put you on a pedestal, use and abuse you, then discard you when there is nothing more they can gain from you. In their minds, you are simply a cog in their wheel of lies. If you catch on to their games, they move on. If not, they take you for everything you have, telling themselves they had to do it to survive, then dismiss you from their minds once you've outlived your usefulness.

Bruce took years grooming me to trust him. People just like Bruce are grooming their next victims at this very minute. Some patiently take years; others take no time before they begin their wicked hidden agenda.

I wish I had seen through Bruce's lies when he started the grooming process the day he told me he *sold* his house, when in fact, he had foreclosed on it and rented a duplex less than a mile from me with a deceitful, ugly scheme in mind. He chose the location purposefully to be near me and my daughter, to win our hearts with his many *thoughtful* yet manipulative tactics.

When I was admiring Bruce's skill as a good listener, I wish I had seen he was purposefully avoiding talking about himself. He quickly learned who I was, what I needed and wanted, and he was eager to fulfill those needs and wants to gain my trust. He was pretending to have a profession, yet he was unable to keep a regular job. He was brilliant, but he chose not to use his mind in a lawful and respectable manner.

I've researched sociopaths and found their brains are wired differently. They lack guilt, empathy, fear, and anxiety. White-collar prison for a short amount of time does nothing to rehabilitate them for reentry back into society, but it happens every day. All they know is to seek out their next victim and repeat the immoral process.

The more naive and trusting you are, the easier it is to become a target, just as I was. Like Bruce, they often choose victims in poor health so they can be their hero. Boundaries, laws, ethics, and moral standards are not a part of their vocabulary.

Although we didn't prove Bruce was poisoning me, I had felt better within days of moving out of the house we shared. I truly believe I am fortunate to be alive. I try not to focus on this thought because it is upsetting. Several of my friends believe Bruce was probably poisoning me with the scheme to use a life insurance policy, unknown to me, which would more than cover the cost of all the extras he was adding to the house. The bank's call, as upsetting as it was, could have saved my life. It haunts me to think what would have happened to Lauren if he'd succeeded.

He was like many sociopaths, staying calm and pretending to have a mild demeanor during the most stressful situations. They will do almost anything to hook their partner and keep them loyal. I wish I had known his empathy and compassion were only part of the scheme to steal everything from me. All the time he spent researching my health issues, searching for cures, pretending to care for me was part of this process. He knew if he won my daughter's heart, I would more likely overlook his lies and ignore his shortcomings.

Once Bruce was caught by the bank, all his kindness, empathy, and compassion evaporated like a puff of smoke. He completely changed into a cruel, mocking shell of what he had been. Bruce was a felon, unable to ever get a loan again. Despite this he immediately found another victim to take advantage of, to groom, to cajole, to steal from. After all, that *is* what sociopaths do. They charm their next victim while running away from their past misdeeds without a care in the world, their conscience clear as the bright blue Oklahoma sky.

Bruce is a sick individual, with many demented behaviors, someone who even with medicine and counseling will never be rehabilitated. Yet he is living among us, free to ruin countless lives, to lie, cheat, and steal from the unsuspecting.

I was compelled to share my story with the hope of helping others who are vulnerable and likely to be taken advantage of as I was. It is the wicked truth there are so many people out there who use God as a tool to whittle their depraved agenda, to use and abuse innocent people without remorse. They use sweet Jesus' name as a weapon to capture their victims' hearts to open another door for their malicious opportunity when they truly have no relationship with Jesus at all. I wish I had only known.

PART 5 – PRESENT DAY

Chapter 49

THANK YOU FOR YOUR SERVICE

DETECTIVE SHEETS

Would I ever feel I could move on from the worry and fear that Bruce planted in my mind? Therapy has helped immensely, and praying for Jesus to heal me has changed my life. As time passes, I have a much healthier frame of mind. I wish I could say PTSD doesn't happen anymore, but that wouldn't be true. I can say, however, that these experiences do not cripple me or take the joy out of my life like they once did, thanks to Jesus.

Recently I was in a clothing store and ran into Detective Sheets, my police detective. I hugged her and she asked how I was doing.

I responded, "Much better than expected. Detective Sheets, I will always be indebted to you for all that you did for Lauren and me. I have a great respect for those in uniform who are seeking justice for people like me, just as you have. You fought for justice."

The detective took my hand and squeezed it. "I'll never forget you. Your case will always remain in the forefront of my mind."

Before we said our goodbyes, I admitted, "Looking back, I wish I'd ordered a background check on Bruce before we were married. It would have saved us both a lot of time and grief."

She nodded. "Good advice."

I shook my head, fighting back emotions. "The truth is, I had a false sense of security since we'd met decades ago. The community loved his family, and he was my dear friend's cousin. I thought I knew him. But I did not know him at all."

Sheets shook her head slowly, knowing too well what I meant. "That is how these people work. They prey on your trust."

I nodded and gathered the courage to tell her something I'd been mulling over for a while now. "I feel compelled to tell other people my story. To urge them to not be naive, especially since sociopaths often prey on trusting, vulnerable women. Even if they go to prison, they are unable to be rehabilitated. They are released quickly and most strike again. Sex offenders are tagged for others to be warned, but sociopaths just reenter society under the radar." I'd never thought I'd be such an easy target for such a sick-minded individual. "My hope is to help others be more careful of those trying to gain their trust."

Nodding her head, she softly smiled and said, "The world needs help."

I shared Jesus' words. "Peace I leave you. My peace I give to you. I do not give to you as the world gives. Do not let your heart be troubled and do not be afraid" (John 14:27 NIV).

Tears welled in my eyes as I hugged her goodbye. God chose her as my detective. His love showed through her dedication to uphold the law, her diligence in finding the truth in our case that was full of deception, and her compassion for my daughter and me. She earned my heartfelt respect and admiration, even to this day. I wish I could repay her for all that she did for us. All I can do is humbly say, "Thank you for your service, Detective Sheets!" I am sure God will bless her greatly.

Chapter 50

JESUS IS THE ONLY KEY

KEYS ARE FULL OF symbolism. They can represent new opportunities, freedom, trust, and respect, like giving a dignitary the keys to the city. Looking back on my past, keys have been intertwined through important events in my life. I vividly remember Daddy looking for his keys the night our house burned. Mom's car keys were inside our burning house, forcing Daddy and Reagan to push her car out of the garage.

The symbolism and deception Bruce used when he proposed to me with a key remains vivid in my mind. I thought it was a key to a new life together, but instead it locked me into a deceitful marriage. He continued to use keys in the psychological games he played, including computer keys he used to wheel, deal, and steal, creating false money market accounts, defrauding the banks, and stealing my hard-earned life savings.

As my world was falling apart, I found keys on the floorboard of my car, keys mysteriously missing from my key chain, only to be returned later in a different order. Some keys were shiny and new, yet I had no idea what they opened. I was shocked when I found out I did not have a key that gave me access to our post office box when he purposely left my name off the account.

When I was feeling the surge of anxiety that my world was collapsing, I kept a special place in *the purse* for my keys, looking for them often just to make sure they were there. Finding them tucked in that pocket of the borrowed purse was one of the few things that helped my anxiety.

Keys are an important part of modern daily life. We've all felt the panic when we lose our keys and look desperately to find them. For me, the key has been trusting Jesus to help me through each day and it has led to real and lasting happiness. He wants to provide stability, peace, unconditional love, grace, and a promise that He will never leave us. We need to allow Him to be the key in our lives and to live in our hearts. We just have to ask Him into our hearts.

Jesus and time are amazing healers. Bruce may have given me a key the night he proposed, but Jesus gave me His heart years ago when I was a little blonde-headed girl, and I gave Him mine. That night I knelt beside my bed in my red and white striped footie pajamas and asked Him to live in my heart. He did not hesitate.

My relationship with Jesus is like no other. He has never betrayed me. He has consistently given me His unconditional love, large doses of tender loving care, a sense of direction, precious amounts of grace, and a security no other can give. Jesus is the only KEY to my life's happiness.

I share my story with you because I am MORE than okay now. I am at peace. Jesus has healed my body and mind. The sluggishness and brain fog I experienced when married to Bruce is gone. I can eat anything I want without suffering. I thank God that the only need to watch what I eat is to control the extra pounds. I've come a long way from years ago when I was sickly, frail, and weighed a mere hundred pounds. I now can enjoy communion, food, fellowship, and parties once again! Jesus has healed my body, my hurt, my disappointment, my loss, and my heart. He is all that I need to feel complete, whole, healthy, and happy. My Savior never left me, and He never will.

Throughout the ordeal, I have found such a blessing and comfort to witness Lauren's faith. She has withstood the storm. Fourteen years later she is a woman of faith and leans on Jesus to help her daily. Sometimes I wonder if it had not been for the storm, would she and I know with all certainty that Jesus is a life raft we can depend on in shallow or deep, treacherous waters. We are thankful that Jesus has always been with us, through the good times and bad.

Jesus wants me to share my story to give hope to you and others, and I truly desire to please Him by encouraging others to accept Him as their Lord and Savior and to lean on Him during the journey of life. No matter what difficulties you will face throughout your life, and we all have those at one time or another, Jesus will help you along the way. He will be your life raft in any storm you face.

I will live the rest of my life forever changed. I will be suspicious, less trusting to a degree, and more careful of those I allow in my inner circle. My radar will forever be changed, but that is not necessarily a bad thing. Seeing the good in others is a quality that pleases Jesus, but He also wants us to guard our hearts.

We read in scripture, "Guard your heart above all else, for it determines the course of your life" (Proverbs 4:23 NLT). Additionally, scripture says, "Getting wisdom is the wisest thing you can do, develop good judgment" (Proverbs 4:7 NLT).

I could have been bitter after Bruce was finally out of our lives, having taken so much from us. I could have let anger feed my soul when the bank foreclosed on our house and I later filed bankruptcy. Darkness and resentment could have taken over my life when I was forced to sell sentimental items to pay the bills. The good credit that I had worked so hard to maintain over the years, even with health issues and a student loan, was stolen from me. I could remain fixated on the day I saw Bruce's glassy eyes in his duplex's garage, hearing his wicked laugh, confirming he had no regret for what he had done to us. But I choose Jesus over bitterness. With that choice, I feel His peace and a joy that only comes from Him.

Without Jesus I probably would still hold anger in my heart, even if I could get over the harm Bruce had done to us. However, it was much more difficult to forgive how he'd hurt Lauren. She loved him, trusted him, and allowed him to be a part of her world. Lauren had been proud of him. Instead of loving her, Bruce stole her money, he stole her senior year, and he broke her heart—*with NO remorse*, a phrase that echoes in my mind. That part is difficult to get past. Without Jesus I would have never forgiven him or forgiven his family for keeping secrets from me.

As we are reminded in the New Testament, "For if you forgive other people when they sin against you, your heavenly Father will also forgive you" (Matthew 6:14 NIV).

I will never understand why my daughter and I were meant to suffer through that time, but I don't dwell on the WHY anymore. I choose to dwell on Jesus. He is the key. He is my key. He wants to be your key. If you open your heart to Jesus, He will never let you down. He is constant, stable, and loving. He is my everything and He wants to be yours, too.

I am thankful for the scriptures in the Bible, and for my Christian friends and family. Blessings have flowed in my life thanks to my parents taking me to church as a child and helping plant "Jesus seeds" in my heart. Who knew, other than Jesus, that I would need Him so badly? Mom and Daddy couldn't have known that what they were rooting would grow into what I desperately depended on thirty years later to get me through my darkest days.

Throughout the last decade of my life, I have continued to rely on scriptures, songs, and visual reminders of Jesus' love. The song "Turn Your Eyes Upon Jesus," written by Helen Lemmel, Aaron Shut, and Paul Baloche, is an extremely powerful reminder of perception. The chorus helps me put life into a healthy perspective:

Turn your eyes upon Jesus,
Look full in His wonderful face,
And the things of Earth will grow strangely dim
In the light of His glory and grace.

There is great truth in the words, "All the things of Earth will grow strangely dim. Look full in His wonderful face." The more I focus on Jesus and His genuine love, the healthier my perspective is about my life's circumstances.

As I have shared, during this storm I became especially fond of these words when Jesus said, "Peace I leave with you; My peace I give to you. I do not give to you as the world gives. Do not let your heart be troubled and do not be afraid" (John14:27 NIV).

I cannot count the many times I have shared this verse with others and said it to myself. It has given me great comfort, as I have felt his peace during the worst of the storm. What a gift Jesus has given us with His word as we seek peace and stability our world does not provide. The truth is, I will never know the real Bruce, but without a doubt I know the real Jesus!

Scripture encourages us, "He heals the brokenhearted and bandages their wounds" (Psalms 147 NLT).

Life is an adventure. Life can sometimes be a storm, yet Jesus is my life raft. I am at peace as I remain in His loving arms. There is no deception; Jesus is THE ONLY KEY!

Chapter 51

THE ENVELOPE SURPRISE

FUNNY THING ABOUT PTSD is it lingers. It can put you right back to your worst moments at the drop of a hat. The day I opened the mailbox and found the letter from Frontier Creek National Bank addressed to both me and Bruce. I hadn't done business with them since I'd been married to Bruce almost a decade and a half ago. I stood dumbfounded. Fourteen years after the crimes he committed, I was staring at our names sharing the same space, my heart beating out of my chest.

I tore the letter open and found an apology to *both of us* for freezing my bank accounts so long ago. Tucked inside was a check for $100, written out to Bruce and Becca Walker. Again, shock hit me seeing our names occupying the same space, especially on a check that had been the cornerstone to his fraudulent behavior. The papers shook, keeping time with my increased heartbeat. This from the bank who years ago told me I could never bank there again even though they knew Bruce was the one at fault.

Was it another one of Bruce's sick jokes? A few phone calls confirmed it was a legitimate check from the bank. Think about this for a minute. The bank that allowed Bruce to steal $2,400 from my frozen accounts when Lauren and I were unable to get even a penny from them?

It made no sense that they sent Bruce, a convicted criminal, money after everything he'd put us through, despite the federal charges brought against him, putting him in prison for sixteen months.

Lauren called me a few hours later. "Mom! You won't believe what I got in the mail today! A letter from the bank and a $100 check with all our names on it! Me, you, and Bruce. Why did they have his name on it too? How did they find my new address? This is sick."

My heart broke for her. We'd both gotten past this horrific period of our lives, and it made me sick we were pulled right back to those miserable days. "It is very sick. I got one too. I'm so sorry you are having to go through this mess all over again. I want to burn them! When will all of this be behind us?"

It felt like Bruce had stalked us all over again. We'd been divorced for close to fourteen years, yet the bank slapped us in the face with an apology for restraints put on the account due to *suspected fraud*.

I walked into the bank holding the envelope, my knees weak with adrenaline. I insisted on seeing the branch manager. The greeter asked if I could give her more information.

All I could muster was, "I have a confidential and upsetting issue."

She looked at me as if she was holding back more questions because of my intensity. She smiled. "I'm sorry, she is out of the office for her lunch hour. Do you want to wait for her or come back?"

I didn't relish the idea of sitting in the bank where I had experienced those traumatic moments. I chose to leave. When I returned a short time later, Dottie Moss, the branch manager, greeted me at the door with a smile.

We made small talk while she walked me back to her office, then after she shut the door, she asked, "How may I help you?"

Taking a deep breath, I handed her the letters and checks, addressed to Lauren, Bruce, and me. I wiped my sweaty palms on my pants, trying to control their shaking. I soaked in the silence as Mrs. Moss read through the documents.

When she was finished, she asked, "What seems to be the problem?"

My voice quivered. I took a deep breath, moved my chair closer to her desk, and explained Bruce's unlawful and deceitful actions that were directly related to her bank. Then I asked her, "Ma'am, how did you get our new mailing addresses?"

Mrs. Moss smiled politely. "It is public knowledge."

Heat rushed to my cheeks, and I was glad I was seated. "Did Bruce receive a check as well?"

"No, we did not have a forwarding address for him," she replied.

"If you had a forwarding address, would you have mailed him a check?" I felt the cooling beads of perspiration on my forehead. "Would Bruce get a check just as my daughter and I did *for any inconvenience*?"

She did not answer.

I filled the silence. "Ma'am, I don't think you understand what I've been through. It was over a decade ago when I got the call from this very bank. I was told if I didn't pay back $24,000 before the end of the business day the case would go to the DA's office. Bruce Walker was my husband at the time. He is now my ex-husband and is a felon due to bank fraud he perpetrated on your bank."

I explained, "The bank's employee, Mrs. Brown, had showed me the three fake money market accounts, two accounts with zero balance, and $707,417 in the third. I'd seen the deposit and withdrawal slips Bruce had written and signed in my name. His handwriting was easily detected, not even trying to duplicate my signature."

Mrs. Moss moved to her computer, capturing my every word about the kited checks from those accounts, then I sat alone in her office as she left to gather more information, made copies of the documents, and came back to find me looking for Kleenex.

Just being back in the bank made me feel dirty. I had moved on with my life, and yet fourteen years later I'd been brought right back to the terrible moment I first found out about Bruce's crimes.

Having to relive it after so much healing and work to put it behind me made my blood boil. I'd done nothing wrong.

Obviously, they had not done their research or else they would have known that Jackson Bruce Walker went to prison for bank fraud connected to their facility.

How badly I wanted to chew her out, saying, "No disrespect, Mrs. Moss, but how ironic that the bank is willing to give him money but yet hadn't thought a second about us when they turned their backs on Lauren and me. Our justice system gave him sixteen months in 'white-collar prison' then released this predator back into the world to find his next victim. It made me realize how broken our system is." Instead, I just bit my tongue and was eager to get out of there.

Mrs. Moss typed quickly, shaking her head while she created a formal complaint to start an investigation. "You may get checks made out to you, without Bruce's name, but there are no guarantees."

I was fuming. The $100 was a joke. "My concern is that my name is still connected to Bruce. If we cashed those checks, the Internal Revenue Service might see us as connected to him. Can't you see that is unacceptable?"

I knew she was in a difficult position and her role was to gather information, empathize to a degree, and minimize this deplorable mishap as much as possible.

When we were finished, I thanked Mrs. Moss for her time, but I looked her in the eye and said, "This facility has put my daughter and me in danger and certainly has upset my world even after fourteen years have passed. Please get to the bottom of this and see that our names have no connection with Jackson Bruce Walker."

Days later I received a call from the investigation division notifying me that the complaint had been received and they would begin working on the case soon.

I explained, "How could you send a check to a felon, to someone who went to prison for the fraud initiated from your bank?"

He answered politely, "It is just standard procedure to add his name to the check because he had been added to your accounts years prior."

"Standard procedure?" Once again, I didn't expect to hear words of apology. That would mean they accepted their responsibility in the matter.

To put salt on the wound, Lauren and I received another letter days later from the bank. They were encouraging us to cash the checks previously received. They had not realized a formal complaint had been filed.

Two weeks later a representative in the investigation department called to share with me, "Ma'am, we were unable to separate your name from Bruce's because you had added his name to your accounts after you married."

I was incredulous. "Just to make sure I am understanding correctly, because we were once married and I added him to my accounts then, no matter what corruption he has chosen to be a part of...your facility will never be able to separate my name from this felon?"

"I'm sorry, ma'am, but this is just standard procedure. The case is now closed. I hope you have a good day." Lauren and I never cashed our $100 checks. They represented a slap in our faces, offering such a small amount after all we had been through.

The words the bank representatives used in every conversation I had questioning them were, "This is standard procedure." Those words will forever be burned in my mind.

EPILOGUE: GOD'S DIVINE MIRACLE

GEORGE MACEY WAS OBEDIENT to God's calling when he awoke at 3:00 a.m. almost fifteen years ago. God audibly told him to pray for Becca Walker. George got out of bed and immediately wrote the name of the stranger on a sticky note so it would not be forgotten. George had never experienced anything like this awakening before or since this once-in-a-lifetime dream.

He and his wife, Leyna, who lived six hours away from where I lived, asked God for more details. What were they to pray for: health, family, a child, a strengthened faith, or something else? God did not reveal any more specifics. They put the sticky note inside a kitchen cabinet and prayed for the stranger every time they saw the note. When the note fell off the cabinet after many years, Leyna taped it back onto the cabinet door. How devoted they were throughout the years to pray for Becca Walker.

Nearly two years ago, I was introduced to George and Leyna in the church sanctuary by one of our mutual friends, Lucy Toner. I quickly felt an unusually strong bond with the couple. They were genuine and caring people who had a strong love for the Lord.

A few months later, I invited Leyna and Lucy to come over to my house after our Bible study. Their genuine compassion for people opened the door to share my recent frustrations over the envelope from the bank with Bruce's name attached to mine.

I didn't couch my emotions. "After all these years, I can't believe they sent that to me! Every time I read Bruce and Becca Walker, my anxiety skyrockets. I thought I was past finding his name on anything alongside mine."

I will never forget the expression on Leyna's face. She inhaled with shock and stared at me with wide eyes. "What was the name you said? Are you *Becca Walker*?"

I replied to my dear friend, "Yes, that was my name when I was married to Bruce fifteen years ago. Why?"

Leyna gripped my arm and whispered, "You aren't going to believe what I am about to tell you." Immediately she called her husband George and asked, "What was the name God gave you when He woke you up so long ago? Wasn't it Becca Walker?"

George didn't hesitate. "Yes! That's the name."

Leyna's voice quivered as she told her husband, "You're not going to believe who Becca Walker is. I'm sitting right beside her. She is our dear friend Becca Bailey!"

Chill bumps covered my entire body, and the hair rose along my neck. George and Leyna had no idea that when they moved to Edmond they would finally meet the lady they had diligently been praying for over the past decade and a half. What a shock to find out I'd been one of their close church friends for months without knowing about George's experience.

I felt an urgency to hug George's neck and thank him for being a faithful prayer warrior for me. Later that afternoon Leyna, George, and I shed many tears together realizing what God had been doing all along behind the scenes. We joined together in a circle and gave God the glory and praised Jesus for orchestrating our friendship so beautifully and purposefully.

The special bond I felt with George and Leyna when I'd first met them was part of God's plan all along. It was not a coincidence. It was God's divine miracle—beyond belief. They'd had no idea I used to be Becca Walker.

When they moved to Edmond, thirteen years after George's dream, they had no idea the church they would be attending was where Becca Walker worshipped. God's plan came full circle as his obedient prayer warriors, George and Leyna, were able to finally meet the woman He had asked them to pray for so long ago.

Recently George found one of his journals. He'd started it when God woke him and put my name on his heart to pray for me. After studying the dates of his journal, he later asked me if a certain month and year were relevant, not knowing the details of my life. Relevant? My whole body shivered. My eyes filled with tears as I remembered my life rapidly unraveling during that dangerous time. It was the same month we had the large bank meeting, when lies were beginning to be revealed. We hugged each other and cried as we felt the presence of the Lord.

I share this story with you because God was there for me in the darkest of days and I survived. He has wanted me to know that He was working in my life even in ways in which I was unaware. He is working in your life as well, whether you realize it or not. He dearly loves each one of his children and you are one of them.

I am so grateful George took His call to pray for me. Looking back at the most dangerous moments my daughter and I lived through, I am certain George and Leyna's prayers for a stranger, along with so many others who prayed for me, were what kept me alive to share this story about Jesus with you.

Knowing where I have been and where I am now, I have no doubt I have experienced miracles of healing in my life. The physical healing and the healing of my broken heart were both miracles from God.

George's faith in prayer mirrored the scripture, "For we walk by faith, not by sight" (2 Corinthians 5:7 KJV). Because of George's obedience to God, God unexpectedly surprised him by answering his prayer to meet Becca Walker one day. He orchestrated our friendship and allowed us to be close before he revealed my name.

I know from my personal experiences, with all certainty, that prayer changes lives. It drastically changed mine. God is always at work whether we are aware of all He does for us or not. Miracles happen sometimes in the most unexpected and unusual ways.

I was beyond frustrated with the bank, but because of their mind-boggling error, Leyna heard me speak my name, the name God had given her husband in the middle of the night. God turned something I felt was horrible into a blessing beyond belief. Scripture reminds us, "And we know that in all things God works for the good of those who love Him, who have been called according to His purpose" (Romans 8:28 NIV). We just have to have our eyes and ears open to His blessings and miracles to experience and appreciate them.

Prayers may be answered immediately, fifteen years later, or not necessarily in our lifetime. You may be blessed with prayers from people you don't even know, as I was. Even if your name isn't on someone's sticky note, Jesus certainly knows your name and has a plan for your life.

Scripture tells us:

"'For I know the plans I have for you,' declares the Lord, 'plans to prosper you and not to harm you, plans to give you hope and a future. Then you will call on Me and come and pray to Me, and I will listen to you. You will seek Me and find Me when you seek Me with all your heart. I will be found by you,' declares the Lord." (Jeremiah 29:11- 14 NIV).

After my experience with George and Leyna, I know I am forever changed. When someone needs me to pray for them, I intend to be obedient. I also have a sticky note inside my kitchen cabinet with George and Leyna's names written on it to be reminded to thank God often for these people who chose to pray for me diligently.

I pray for you, as you have this book in your hands, that it will change your life. I pray that you will be helped in some way. May protection and blessings flow over you, and may you have faith in Jesus because He loves you like *no one else ever will.*

In Jesus' name. Amen.

The End

ACKNOWLEDGEMENTS

Many people have encouraged me during the process of writing this book. Without them I know I would not have completed the task God put on my heart long ago. I would much rather be doing just about anything than reliving my past.

I would like to thank Mrs. J, who read the first drafts and pushed me along the way. KW was amazing as she did her magic and polished my rough edges. KK has been my consistent and enthusiastic cheerleader who has always believed in me. Countless dedicated friends have prayed for me through this in hopes my story would help others.

ABOUT THE AUTHOR

I once was a naïve and trusting person who believed people had pure hearts and good intentions. That all changed the day my ex-husband's demented character was finally revealed to me. How I wish I had known the red flags of danger to look for in the man I was giving my heart to. Soon after the truth was evident, I leaned on my faith to help save me and my daughter from more harm in the darkest chapters of our lives.

Being married to a sociopath quickly unraveled my heart, yet Jesus healed me. I can finally enjoy laughing again. Spending quality time with friends and family in my inner circle brings me joy, something I thought I'd lost in the worst of the ordeal. You can now find me outside in the sunshine, gardening, crafting, cooking, and playing games.

It has been a fifteen-year journey to write my story, something God put on my heart long ago to do. I pray that it helps others protect themselves and those they love from the pain my daughter and I endured.